GW01376873

FRACTALS

NEW & SELECTED POEMS | TRANSLATIONS 1980–2015

SUDEEP SEN [www.sudeepsen.net] is widely recognised as a major new generation voice in world literature and "one of the finest younger English-language poets in the international literary scene" (*BBC Radio*). He is "fascinated not just by language but the possibilities of language" (*Scotland on Sunday*). He read English Literature at the University of Delhi and as an Inlaks Scholar received an MS from the Journalism School at Columbia University (New York). His awards, fellowships & residencies include: Hawthornden Fellowship (UK), Pushcart Prize nomination (USA), BreadLoaf (USA), NLPVF Dutch Foundation for Literature (Amsterdam), Ledig House (New York), Sanskriti (New Delhi), Wolfsberg UBS Pro Helvetia (Switzerland), Tyrone Guthrie Centre (Ireland), Shanghai Writers Programme (China), AsiaLink Bookwallah (India/Australia), and the 'Pleiades' honour at the 2004 Struga Poetry Festival for having made "a significant contribution to contemporary world poetry" (Macedonia). He was international writer-in-residence at the Scottish Poetry Library (Edinburgh) and visiting scholar at Harvard University.

Sen's critically-acclaimed books include *The Lunar Visitations, New York Times, Dali's Twisted Hands, Postmarked India: New & Selected Poems* (HarperCollins), *Distracted Geographies, Prayer Flag, Rain, Aria* (A K Ramanujan Translation Award), *Ladakh, Blue Nude* (Jorge Zalamea International Poetry Prize), *Fractals: New & Selected Poems|Translations 1980-2015* and *EroText*. He has also edited several important anthologies, including *The HarperCollins Book of English Poetry, World English Poetry, Prairie Schooner Feast Anthology of Indian Women's Poetry, Another English Poetry Foundation Anthology, Poetry Review Centrefold of Indian Poems, The Literary Review Indian Poetry, World Literature Today Writing from Modern India, The Yellow Nib Modern English Poetry by Indians, Midnight's Grandchildren: Post-Independence English Poetry from India, Wasafiri New Writing from India, South Asia & the Diaspora*, and, *Lines Review Twelve Modern Young Indian Poets*.

His poems, translated into over twenty-five languages, have featured in international anthologies by Penguin, Random House, HarperCollins, Bloomsbury, Routledge, Norton, Knopf, Everyman, Macmillan, and Granta. His words have appeared in the *Times Literary Supplement, Newsweek, Guardian, Observer, Independent, Telegraph, Financial Times, Herald, London Magazine, Poetry Review, Literary Review, Harvard Review, Hindu, Hindustan Times, Times of India, Indian Express, Outlook, India Today*, and broadcast on BBC, PBS, CNN IBN, NDTV, AIR & *Doordarshan*. Sen's newer work appears in *New Writing 15* (Granta), *Language for a New Century* (Norton), *Leela: An Erotic Play of Verse and Art* (Collins), *Indian Love Poems* (Knopf/Random House/Everyman), *Out of Bounds* (Bloodaxe), and *Initiate: Oxford New Writing* (Blackwell). He is the editorial director of AARK ARTS and the editor of *Atlas*. [www.atlasaarkarts.net]

As a photographer, his images are part of international art fairs, exhibitions, print portfolios, and private collections. His art photographs have been published in leading magazines and newspapers, on book jacket covers, record labels, and online such as *NationalGeographic*.com. Sen's photography is professionally represented by ArtMbassy in Berlin.

Sudeep Sen is the first Asian to be honoured with an invitation to participate at the 2013 Nobel Laureate Week in St Lucia, where he delivered the Derek Walcott Lecture and read his own poetry. At that occasion, a commemorative limited edition, *Fractals: New & Selected Poems|Translations 1978-2013*, was released by the Nobel laureate himself. The same year, the Government of India's Ministry of Culture awarded him the senior fellowship for "outstanding persons in the field of culture/literature".

Works by Sudeep Sen

POETRY | FICTION | NON-FICTION
[Books | Chapbooks | CDs | E-books]
Leaning Against the Lamppost; The Man in the Hut; The Lunar Visitations; Kali in Ottava Rima; New York Times; Parallel: Selected Poems; South African Woodcut; Mount Vesuvius in Eight Frames; Dali's Twisted Hands; Postmarked India: New & Selected Poems; BodyText; Retracing American Contours; Almanac; Lines of Desire; A Blank Letter; Perpetual Diary; Postcards from Bangladesh; Monsoon; The Single Malt; Prayer Flag; Distracted Geographies: An Archipelago of Intent; Rain; Rainbow; Heat; Winter; Ladakh; Blue Nude; Kargil; Fractals: New & Selected Poems | Translations 1980-2015; EroText

DRAMA
[Radio | Stage]
Vesuvius *(London: BBC Radio)*, Vesuvius *(London: Border Crossing)*, BodyText *(London: Border Crossing)*, Rain *(New Delhi: British Council & Mumbai: Kala Ghoda Arts Festival)*, Wo|Man *(New Delhi: India International Centre)*, T3 *(New Delhi: The Attic)*, Rain *(New Delhi: India International Centre)*

FILM
[Short Feature | Documentary]
Rhythm, White Shoe Story, Woman of a Thousand Fires, Babylon is Dying: Diary of Third Street, Flying Home & others

TRANSLATION
[Books | Chapbooks | Films]
In Another Tongue; Hayat Saif: Selected Poems; Love & Other Poems by Aminur Rahman; Spellbound & Other Poems by Fazal Shahabuddin; Love Poems by Shamsur Rahman; Aria|Anika, The Single Malt, Rain, Banyan, Mediterranean, Offering, Indian Dessert, Incarnadine, Elegy for Delhi, Derek Walcott: Poetry is an Island

EDITOR
[Books | Journals | E-zine]
Lines Review Twelve Modern Young Indian Poets; Wasafiri Contemporary Writings from India, South Asia & the Diaspora; Index on Censorship Songs [Poems] of Partition; Biblio Portfolio of South Asian Poetry; The British Council Book of Emerging English Poets from Bangladesh; Dash: Four New German Writers; Sestet; Modern English Poetry from Bangladesh; Midnight's Grandchildren: Post-Independence English Poetry from India; The Literary Review Indian Poetry, The Yellow Nib Modern English Poetry by Indians, World Literature Today Writing from Modern India, Another English Poetry Foundation Anthology, Poetry Review Centrefold of Indian Poems, Prairie Schooner Feast Anthology of Indian Women's Poetry, Atlas, The HarperCollins Book of English Poetry, World English Poetry

Fractals | SUDEEP SEN
NEW & SELECTED POEMS | TRANSLATIONS 1980-2015

Sudeep Sen

*For Mohim —
So lovely to see you
in Londistan — See
you in Delhi —
S. June 7, 2016*

LONDON MAGAZINE EDITIONS

Published in the United Kingdom by
LONDON MAGAZINE EDITIONS
The London Magazine
11 Queen's Gate
LondonSW7 5EL
United Kingdom
www.thelondonmagazine.org

Copyright 2016 © Original Poems & Translations by SUDEEP SEN
Copyright 2016 © Non-English Poems by Individual Poets
Copyright 2016 © Author Photo by ARIA SEN
Copyright 2016 © Cover Photo by CAMILLE LIZARRIBAR

ISBN: 978-0-9926061-7-6 (Hardback)
ISBN: 978-0-9926061-8-3 (Paperback)
ISBN: 978-0-9926061-9-0 (E-book/Kindle)

A catalogue record for this book is available from the
British Library.

All rights reserved. This book contains material protected under International and Federal Copyright Laws and Treaties. Any unauthorised reprint or use of this material is prohibited. No part of this book maybe used or reproduced in any manner whatsoever without the written permission of the publisher and author except in the case of quotations embodied in critical articles or reviews.

Typeset in Adobe Caslon Pro, Arial & Scriptina 10/12 pts.
Book & cover master design by Sudeep Sen
www.sudeepsen.net | www.atlasaarkarts.net

※

Fractals contains a selection of over 250 new poems and translations composed between 1998 and 2015. It also includes a batch of about 50 odd poems from the 1997 out-of-print volume — *Postmarked India: New & Selected Poems* (HarperCollins) — that have been frequently reprinted, anthologised and taught.

 Grateful thanks to Jane Draycott, Jenny Lewis, Lesley Saunders, Kim Morrissey, Leona Medlin, Peggy Herring, Tulsi Badrinath and Bryce Milligan for their close reading, insightful comments and deft edits. For the UK edition, many thanks to Carol Ann Duffy, Fiona Sampson, Elaine Feinstein, Maureen Duffy, Steven O'Brien and Rachel Chanter. And to Rama Nair and Shormishtha Panja for their two excellent books of critical studies of my work.

 My deepest gratitude to Joseph Brodsky, Yehuda Amichai, Peter Porter, John Hartley Williams and Kwame Dawes — who over various phases of my writing career — helped select the contents that ultimately gave shape to this book. And finally, a very special thank you to Sigrid Nama & Derek Walcott.   — S.S.

> *Gods came tumbling down
> in Bhaktapur. Everest
> churned — snow, debris, death.*
> — s.s., 'Kathmandu Earthquake'
> *The London Magazine*

for
DEREK & JOSEPH

🌀

*Ah, but a man's reach should exceed his grasp,
Or what's a Heaven for?*
— ROBERT BROWNING, *Andrea Del Sarto*

I think poetry is a fundamental human activity, and must continue. I think the minute we stop writing poetry, or reading it, we cease being human.
— MARK STRAND, 'The Art of Poetry No. 77', *The Paris Review*

*Poets are poetry, writers are prose — //
Prose can hold anything including poetry,
but in poetry, there's only room for poetry —*
— WISLAWA SZYMBORSKA, 'Stage Fright'

FRACTAL

fractal [(frak-tl)]
noun, Mathematics, Physics.
a geometrical or physical structure having an irregular or fragmented shape at all scales of measurement between a greatest and smallest scale such that certain mathematical or physical properties of the structure, as the perimeter of a curve or the flow rate in a porous medium, behave as if the dimensions of the structure (fractal dimensions) are greater than the spatial dimensions.

Word Origin
fractal
1975, from Fr., from L. fractus "broken," pp. of frangere "to break" (see fraction). Coined by Fr. mathematician Benoit Mandelbrot in "Les Objets Fractals."

Source: *Online Etymology Dictionary*, © 2010 Douglas Harper. All rights reserved.

Science Dictionary
fractal [(frāk'təl)] complex geometric pattern exhibiting self-similarity in that small details of its structure viewed at any scale repeat elements of the overall pattern. See more at chaos.

Cultural Dictionary
fractal [(frak -tuhl)]
Contraction of "fractional dimension." This is a term used by mathematicians to describe certain geometrical structures whose shape appears to be the same regardless of the level of magnification used to view them. A standard example is a sea coast, which looks roughly the same whether viewed from a satellite or an airplane, on foot, or under a magnifying glass. Many natural shapes approximate fractals, and they are widely used to produce images in television and movies.

Source: *The American Heritage® New Dictionary of Cultural Literacy, Third Edition* Copyright © 2005 by Houghton Mifflin Company. Published by Houghton Mifflin Company. All rights reserved.

CONTENTS

INTRODUCTION: The Delicacy of Proximity | 19

1 NEWER POEMS [1998—2015]

1. FRACTALS

Mediterranean | 25
Banyan | 26
Winter | 27
Choice | 28
Rabindranath Tagore | 29
    Erasure | 29
    Self-Portrait | 29
    Song | 29
Chinese Calligraphy | 30
Ophelia: Bacterial Fragments | 34
Grammar | 35
Lily Pads | 36
Aorta Art | 39
Matrix | 40
Innocence | 41
Goa Haiku | 42
Tongue: Diptych | 44
New Public Library | 47
Safe | 48
Raghu Rai Photograph | 50

2. BODYTEXT

Magnetising Dead Bones | 53
Wishbones, Arias, Memories | 55
Fever Pitch | 57
Heavy Water | 59
'O' Zone | 60
Night Ward | 61
Icicles | 61
Photons, Graphite, Blood | 62
Rural Mappings | 64
Postcards | 66

3. Variations on Waka

1. Banyan | Stills from Sanskriti

Star Glass | 71
Leaf on Water | 71
Arch | 71
Mustard | 72
Barahkhamba | 72
Centre | 73
Gaon | 73
Iris | 73
Shape | 73
Amaltas | 74
Haveli | 74
Installation | 74

4. Ladakh

1. Ladakh

Zoji La Pass | 77
Drypoint Plates | 78
Zanskar-Indus Valley | 79
Kargil | 80
Drass | 82
Magnetic Hill | 83
Gompa | 84
Chant | 85
Indus | 86
Prayer Flag *(reprise)* | 87
Snow Struck | 88

2. Prayer Flag

Prayer Flag | 90

5. Rain

Rain, Maps | 97
Rain, Rain | 98
Languor, Wet | 98
Fern Frost | 99
Air-Conditioner, Rain | 100
Heavy Metal | 101
Monsoon Greens | 102

Bengal Rain | 102
Rain Charm | 103
Night Rain | 103
Shower, Wake | 104
Drought, Cloud | 104
Knowledge, Need | 104

6. EroText:
SIXTEEN MOVEMENTS ON EROTICA

Indian Dessert | 107
Desire | 107
Absences | 108
Taste | 108
Lying Bare | 109
Morning | 110
Day Before Summer Solstice | 110
Kiss | 110
Sketch | 110
Climax | 111
Release | 111
Longing | 112
Glued | 112
After Sunday Breakfast | 113
Want | 113
Rain | 114

7. Wo|Man

1. Wo|Man

Heather | 117
Feminine Musk | 118
Carole | 119
Gold Squares on Muslin | 120
White | 124
Blue | 126
Silence | 127

2. Whispering Anklets

Mohiniyattam | 128
Bharatanatyam Dancer | 129
Odissi | 130
Almost a Touch | 131

Dedication | 132
Separation | 134

8. BLUE NUDE

1. Dreaming of Cézanne

The Cardplayers | 137
The Skulls | 138
Jacket on the Chair | 140

2. Picasso Triptych

Head I | 141
Head II | 142
Head III | 143

3. Matisse Sequence

Woman with Amphora | 144
Woman with Amphora and Pomegranates | 145
Creation | 146
Standing Blue Nude | 146
Sati | 147
Sine Curve | 148
Blue Nude Skipping Rope | 149
Blue Nude I | 150
Blue Nude II | 151
Blue Nude III | 152
Blue Nude IV | 153

4. Canvas

Four Watercolours | 154
  Railway Station, Bombay | 154
  Lodi Gardens, Delhi | 155
  Udaipur, Rajasthan | 156
  Elm Park Lane, London | 157
Dali's *Pâte de Verre* | 158
Drawing Kafka Out | 159
Chagall Chancel | 160
Amistad | 161
Roté Fabrik Paintings | 162
Cover Drawing | 164
Cow-Dust Hour | 167
English Colours | 168

Shadows of Black | 170
Moth, Art | 170
Triptych³: Feast | 171
Acrylic | 172

5. White Balance

Anish Kapoor | 174
Yuki | 176
Saint Sebastian | 177
Red Rain | 178
The Vortex | The Journey to the Centre of the Earth | 179
Iris | 180
August Rhapsody | 181

6. Mixed Media

Freehold | Leasehold | 182
Entropy | 184
Your Flight | 186

9. GEOGRAPHIES

1. Hawthornden Suite (extracts)

Caves | 189
Castle Walk | 190
Dungeon | 192

2. Crossing Tongues

Crossing Tongues | 193
Ledig Notes | 194

3. Distracted Geographies (extracts)

Graveyard | 198
Church Notes | 199

4. Macedonian Triptych

Night Shot, Krusevo | 201
River Drim, Struga | 202
White Boats, Lake Ohrid | 203

5. Nile Songs

Visiting Cavafy | 204
Nile Songs on Felucca Sails | 205
Alexandria | 206
Shattered Shelters | 207
Mediterranean | 25

6. Crossing the Liffey

Electric Text | 208
Searching for Seamus | 209
Changing Hands | 211
Guinness | 212
Ballynahinch | 213

7. The Wailing Wall

The Wailing Wall | 214
The Wailing Wall, Revisited | 215
Desert Triptych | 218
   Spring in the Desert: I | 218
   Spring in the Desert: II | 218
   Spring in the Desert: III | 219
Diaspora | 220
At Pesto Cafe | 221
Carving Salmon | 222
Israeli Airwaves | 223
Circumcision | 224
Almaya, Jaffa | 226
Reading with the Wind | 228

10. PRAYER CALL

1. Heat

Prayer Call: Heat | 231
Eating Rice & Fish | 237

2. Offering

Aria's Footprint | 238
Bowl | 240
Striking Matches | 242

Neck[lace] | 244
Novæmber | 245
Sahara | 246
Mirrorwork | 247
Offering | 248
February 28¼ | 249
Heat | 250

11. Facsimile (extracts)

Light in my Study | 253
Sun-Blanched Blood | 254
Eating Guavas outside Taj Mahal | 256
Dialogue|Cricket | 257

12. Elegies

Dadu | 261
Suspended Particles | 262
During the Street Play | 263
Gaza | 265
MH-17 Crash | 265
Elegy for Delhi: 29/10 | 266
Baba|Father | 268
Ma|Mother | 270
Mother | 270

13. Gaayika'r Chithi:
notes from a singer's scoresheet

Bideshini/Banalata | 273
Jessore | 274
Delhi | 274
Dhaka | 275
Nowadays | 275
Winter Evening | 276
Remembrance | 278
Question | 279
Shiuli | 280

2 SELECTED EARLIER POEMS [1980—1997]

1. Parsing

Single Malt | 283
Flying Home | 284
A Blank Letter | 285
Mermaid Purse | 286
The Photograph | 288
Fragmented Feathers and Transparent Bones | 290
Rhyme Royal for an Ancient Chinese Wine | 291
Old Room | 292

2. Sexless like Alphabets

1. New York Times

New York Times | 295
Rain on Hot Concrete | 296
Scattered Pieces of a Quarrel | 297
Sun Streaks on Telephone Lines | 298
Night in Times Square | 299
Sexless like Alphabets | 300
Inside Closed Eyes, Even the Stones Come Alive | 301
Sulphur | 302

2. Retracing American Contours

Birch | 303
Penumbra | 304
A Tumbleweed | 305
The Dancing Ground | 306
Scapula, Skulls & Twisted Bones | 307
Ancient Mariner: An Unfinished Story | 308
Bridal Veil Falls | 309
Valley of the Gods | 310
Cumulonimbus | 312

3. BRIEF|CASE

1. Colour Bar | South African Woodcut

Colour Bar | 315
Independent Homeland |315
Durban | 315
Rosary of Waves | 316
Feathers of Snow | 316
97 6th Avenue, Mayfair | 317
South African Woodcut | 318
Dargle Valley, Midlands Meander | 319

2. Half Light

Dali's Twisted Hands | 320
April's Air | 321
Museé D'Orsay, Paris | 322

4. THE ACHE OF THE ARCHIVIST

Remembering Hiroshima Tonight | 325
One Moonlit December Night | 326
Conceit | 326
Ducks | 326
Neonic Cocktail | 327
The Fall Out | 327
The Man in the Hut | 328
The Asylum | 329
Woman of a Thousand Fires | 331
Leaning Against the Lamp-Post | 332
The Tin Can | 335

5. INDIA INK

Kali in [Double] Ottava Rima | 339
Lord Jagannath | 339
Durga Puja | 340
A Pilgrimage to Mathura | 342
Govind Dev Temple, Vrindavan | 343
The Box-Office Hit | 344
Calcutta | Kolkata | 345
August 9, 1964 | 346

Villanelle Variation for Shiva | 347
Sun's Golden Sands | 348
Translating Poetry | 350

6. VESUVIUS

Mount Vesuvius in Eight Frames | 353

3 SELECTED TRANSLATIONS [1997—2015]

1. Bengali

JIBANANANDA DAS
Banalata Sen | 361

RABINDRANATH TAGORE
'In school, yawns' | 362
'In Kanchrapara' | 362
'Two ears pierced' | 363
'Bird-seller says, "This is a black-coloured chanda."' | 363

MANDAKRANTA SEN
A Letter from Lesbos | 364

MITHU SEN
Magpie, Sparrow | 364

SHAMSUR RAHMAN
Love's Overture | 365

AMINUR RAHMAN
Love: 5 | 365

FAZAL SHAHABUDDIN
Spellbound | 366

2. Hindi & Urdu

KAIFI AZMI
One Kiss | 367

GULZAR
Sketch | 367
Ash | 367

SACHCHIDANANDA VATSYAYAN AGYEYA
Sunset | 368

ATAL BIHARI VAJPAYEE
Pain | 368

KAILASH VAJPEYI
Make a Way | 368

KUNWAR NARAIN
Question | 369

ASHOK VAJPEYI
Play | 369

SHAMSHER SINGH BAHADUR
'An empty lonely path, a sad waterfall' | 369

RATI SAXENA
Feast Time | 370

SAVITA SINGH
Woman is Truth | 370

KEDARNATH SINGH
Self-Portrait | 371

MANGALESH DABRAL
Touch | 372

ANAMIKA
Salt | 373

3. In Another Tongue

MOON CHUNG HEE
Willow | 374

CAI TIANXIN
Boston | 374

AVRAHAM BEN YITSHAK
The Lonely Say | 375

AMIR OR
Archer | 375

SHIRIN RAZAVIAN
It is Winter | 376

DITTE STEENSBALLE
There Lies | 376

ZORAN ANCHEVSKI
My Little Me | 377

PETKO DABESKI
Moments and Moment | 377

EWA SONNENBERG
On the Shore | 378

VERONICA ARANDA
XV | 378

MATTEO CAMPAGNOLI
from In Spain | 379

SERGIO LIMA
The Body [of a Woman] Signifies | 380

COLOPHON

Author Note | 383
Publishers' Note | 383
About the Type | 383
Acknowledgements | 384
Dedications | 384
Thank You | 385
London Magazine History | 388
London Magazine Editions | 390

INTRODUCTION

THE DELICACY OF PROXIMITY

> Poised, elegantly constructed poems ....
> — CAROL ANN DUFFY

> A fine contemporary voice whose work is simultaneously urgent, intelligent, innovative, crafted and lyrical.
> — PETER PORTER

SUDEEP SEN is a truly international poet. In the era of globalisation, he has responded to the challenges of the connected world with a unique poetic synthesis. No other poet writing in English today manages to balance the steely North American tradition with the lyric sincerity to be found in much of the rest of the world, from the subcontinent to Europe and beyond. Sen responds uniquely to the artistic opportunities that have been opened up by the new global cultures.

Sen's unusually creative response to our rapidly changing world makes him both innovative and exemplary. But this is not to forget that he is also simply a very fine, highly imagistic poet; one who produces such brilliant, tightly stitched pictures as the 'Shadow' from his 'Goa Haiku' series —

> glittering sea-skin
>   at mid-day, shadow-dance on
> flint-speckled sand dunes

— or who notes, in one of many fine ekphrastic poems, the way Henri Matisse's 'Femme à l'amphore et grenades' appears: "Having stolen / the blue / from the sky's / canvas / for her own body". Sen works particularly with French modernist masters, Matisse, Picasso and Cezanne, but also with Dali and with contemporary artists including Anish Kapoor. *Blue Nude,* his ekphrastic series, beautifully judges how to exceed the given of the original painting by taking its own descriptions into confessional, emotional realms.

Alongside this brilliant, and often emotive, colouration, Sen also conjures swoops of insight. In 'English Colours':

> Suburbia's quiet pastels,
>   its silent music
> make me restless.
>
> I go out for a walk,
>   there is more beauty
> in the grey cold rains.

The characteristic flow of sentences across the short Sen line is what allows us to experience the poem as "swooping" on the insight like a raptor, or a camera shot zooming in suddenly. The motion is hugely fluent. Here it comes again, in one of the opening poems, 'Banyan':

> alphabets
>
> for a calligrapher's
>   nib
>
> italicised
>   in invisible ink,
>
> letters never
>   posted,
>
> cartographer's
>   map, uncharted —
>
> as phrases fold
>   so do veils.

Momentum allows the sense to cohere, so that the concluding insight feels "natural".

In later poems the rhythmic "scoring" of the beautifully enjambed Sen phrase and line is sometimes more horizontal than the sheer vertical drop of these poems. At times this horizontality even stretches into prose poetry. In a piece like 'Ledig Notes', however, the spaces and the punctuation create the music of thought:

> The untarred road sweeps its gravel in a rowdy grey arc.
> It rains, and then stops — the wet
> glaze mourns for light.
> At night it is freezing — shingles turning into irregular
> eroded ice-rocks.

But this rhythmically choreographed insight has also been constructed by and through *images*. His thinking-with-pictures makes Sen's poetry uniquely vivid and accessible. There is a grammar to his images that allows him to build with them. His colours have associations with moods, for example; lists accumulate; while the associations of memory are often transformed into metaphors.

At the same time, a *rhythmic* connectedness both springs from and enables these connections. Both sense-connection and aural-connectedness keep the verse in motion. The poetry is filmic rather than simply pictorial. This too marks Sen as a pioneer of the digital era. His world is animate: one thing connects with another, as one thought connects to the next. We can always click through to the next link, his images suggest. Yet their fluency and beauty prevents any hint of a purely mechanistic post-modernism. We may live *post modernity*, in a world to which fluency and the contemporary, given moment have come flooding back. But this doesn't make us subject to merely arbitrary connections with the world of everything. Instead, Sen is highly discriminating. He is interested in light, landscape, love and desire, as well as in the visual sense in which these poems are bathed.

So we return to the creative syntheses that make Sudeep Sen such an international poet. His poetics brilliantly synthesise the resources of contemporary North American and European writing with the traditions of writing in English from the Indian subcontinent. For example, from the last of these come, among other things, his interest in the flexibility of free verse, his abundant visual imagery, and the risks he takes with straightforward beauty. From the British tradition comes a literality of diction — there's none of the throat-clearing of some North American "cool": these poems "own" their own experiences and emotions. Many British traditions also go by way of the concrete particular to the abstract insight, as does Sen. North American poetics are perhaps the most hospitable to risk and range such as Sen's, and also to a certain swept-clean diction: a poetry of intellection rather than song. Perhaps particularly North American, too, is the rich density of the epigraphs he employs: though the range of reading they reveal isn't confined to a single country, or even hemisphere.

Of course, he is also an international poet in the traditional sense of having a distinguished international reputation: his work is published, translated and honoured across the world. Moreover, the places and cultures he writes about are located in every continent. *Fractals* is, among other things, a book to make the reader long to travel.

There is one other fascinating aspect to Sen's poetics of internationalism. He is exceptionally interested in boundaries. These poems are alive to their possibilities, and preoccupied with the delicacy of proximity. Often the boundary is human skin. In *EroText*, that skin is "bristling, burning, // breaking into sweats of desire", while in 'Odissi', from another erotically-charged sequence, *Wo/Man*, the narrator is moved by a dancer but, "I can only trace imaginary lines with my human hands on the stage's black canvas". Sometimes the boundary that is or is not quite crossed is the space between ink and the white page. Sometimes, whether or not it goes by way of images of paper and skin, the boundary is perception itself. Sen's poetic persona encourages us, as he encourages himself, to go forwards and, with extreme care and delicacy, to encounter something beyond ourselves and what we know. It is a surprising, and beautifully apt, image for the globally connected world:

> there is tactility in the vanishing
> point,
> the point is
> a pointillist's vision, bullet marked, beautiful —
> a deftly deranged love.
> (from 'Ledig Notes')

— FIONA SAMPSON
Frampton on Severn, April 30th 2016

1.
FRACTALS

*Etched away from / the ray-shot wind of your language /
… the hundred-/tongued pseudo-/poem, the noem.*
— PAUL CELAN, 'Etched Away From'

consolatory asymptote
— CHARLES BERNSTEIN, 'Space and Poetry'

*Language is a skin: I rub my language against each other.
It is as if I had words instead of fingers, or fingers at the tip of my
words. My language trembles with desire.*
— ROLAND BARTHES

1 NEWER POEMS [1998—2015]

MEDITERRANEAN

    1

A bright red boat
Yellow capsicums

Blue fishing nets
Ochre fort walls

    2

Sahar's silk blouse
gold and sheer

Her dark black
kohl-lined lashes

    3

A street child's
brown fists

holding the rainbow
in his small grasp

    4

My lost memory
white and frozen

now melts colour
ready to refract

Alexandria

BANYAN

As winter secrets
   melt

with the purple
   sun,

what is revealed
   is electric —

notes tune
   unknown scales,

syntax alters
   tongues,

terracotta melts
   white,

banyan ribbons
   into armatures

as branch-roots
   twist, meeting

soil in a circle.
   Circuits

glazed
   under cloth

carry
   alphabets

for a calligrapher's
   nib

italicised
   in invisible ink,

letters never
   posted,

cartographer's
    map, uncharted —

as phrases fold
    so do veils.

❧

WINTER

Couched on crimson cushions,
    pink bleeds gold

and red spills into one's heart.
    Broad leather keeps time,

calibrating different hours
    in different zones

unaware of the grammar
    that makes sense.

Only random woofs and snores
    of two distant dogs

on a very cold night
    clears fog that is unresolved.

New plants wait for new heat —
    to grow, to mature.

An old cane recliner contains
    poetry for peace — woven

text keeping comfort in place.
    But it is the impatience of want

that keeps equations unsolved.
    Heavy, translucent, vaporous,

split red by mother tongues —
    winter's breath is pink.

CHOICE

drawing a breath between each
*   sentence, trailing closely every word.*
*   — JAMES HOCH, 'Draft' in* Miscreants

1.

some things, I knew,
    were beyond choosing:

didu — grandmother — wilting
        under cancer's terminal care.

mama — my uncle's — mysterious disappearance —
        ventilator vibrating, severed
silently, in the hospital's unkempt dark.

an old friend's biting silence — unexplained —
    promised loyalties melting for profit
        abandoning long familial presences of trust.

devi's jealous heart   misreading emails
        hacked carefully under cover,
her fingernails ripping
unformed poems, bloodied, scarred —
        my diary pages weeping wordlessly —
my children aborted, breathless forever.

2.

these are acts that enact themselves, regardless —
    helpless, as i am,
torn asunder permanently, drugged, numbed.

strange love, this is —   *a salving:*
    what medics and nurses do.

i live buddha-like, unblinking, a painted vacant smile —
                one that stores pain and painlessness —
someone else's nirvana thrust upon me.

some things i once believed in
                              are *beyond* my *choosing* —
choosing is a choice unavailable to me.

༈

RABINDRANATH TAGORE
haiku triptych

ERASURE

lines of poems
   scratched out, erased to ink in —
new shapes — art revealed

SELF-PORTRAIT

gouache shade's matt-blur —
   an outline of the psyche —
subtle peek into soul's eye

SONG

rabindra sangeet's
   nasal baritone — honey-
tinged, monotonic

CHINESE CALLIGRAPHY

Wolf and sheep hair
   gather arcs, jet-black

ink, looped character
   ideograms —

a lifetime of words,
   wisdom, history.

Elegant brush-tips,
   sharpened to a point

by water's healing touch,
   sable-hair stroked

to an elliptical gathering
   of fine-graded hair

end in a finite point,
   a pliable nib

controlling serif-strokes,
   depending upon

the hand's subtle
   human-weight.

Some brushes
   have carved heads

containing the sound
   of pigeons —

ancient postmen,
   now a cosmetic

gaggle of bird-talk.
   Yet others,

mere bamboo-stalks
   sharpened, carved,

bearing the name
   of a poet,

or a phrase
   from a poem,

or even the place
   it was made.

Characters'
   incipient moon-birth,

their lunar image
   a slow-transforming

complex matrix,
   a grid of lines

and strokes —
   cursive, traditional,

clerical, modern.
   Ink's history

from chalk and water
   to ready-made

solution
   does not always rely

on the round
   and oval stones —

mixing plates —
   where

circles and crescents
   collide,

dots, streaks
   and lines meet,

appearing and
   disappearing

depending on the ink's
   fluid strength.

Root of a tree
   holds brushes at rest,

and part of the
    trunk, now carved,

flattens hand-made
    cream felt

and white rice-paper
    into translucent tablets,

perfect empty sheets —
    tabula rasa.

The slow glide of
    a wet brush,

delicately swathed
    in deep-black ink,

our fingers
    calibrating

the characters'
    gentle touch

tell a story
    that is both

apparent and hidden
    to an everyday eye.

Music of its sweep,
    length, breadth —

the broadening
    and narrowing

of brush-strokes
    are human emotions —

mood-swings
    that make up

the story as a whole.
    Lyrics, latent,

embedded beautifully —
    describe a score,

understated,
    yet bold

in its intention.
    Brush-tips sing

as moisture
    evaporates.

Then they are washed
    clean, wrapped

in knitted bamboo-mats,
    hung out to dry

for the next inspiration
    to catch flight.

Black chalk and water
    rubbed on stone

will now have to wait,
    until the next

peony blossoms bloom.
    The final touch —

an artist's signature,
    an autograph,

a stamp
    carved on stone —

pressed on oily-ink,
    blood-red —

incarnadine —
    leaving secret clues

in the corner
    of a page,

a story that'll unravel
    and sing, next spring.

Shanghai 2011

OPHELIA: BACTERIAL FRAGMENTS

Ophelia floats
      buoyant in sub-aqua blue —
her heartbeat
      like the waning and waxing of the moon
or the appearance and disappearance of the sun —

She is the queen of penumbra —

She is not a mother, daughter, sister, or a friend —
        she is a lover, a lover of all
    who can unveil
the beautiful bacterial colours
      without a microscope or lens.

Blue-green Lethe — looping lines —
      wondrous incandescent
"river of regret".
Kelp keeps herself elastic and moist and ready
      breathing virus —
vacuum-bubbles whispering:
        "Does Ophelia have cold feet?"
Blue-green veins leave imprints
    insoluble in water, in air, on skin.

"The person you are calling is waiting,
is waiting, ... not waiting."
        Two moon-beams
    like tiny talismanic   oval stones
move in an arc — an elliptical orbit —
    the lumen alterations
calibrate
    her breath of death,
        breath of love,   a lover —
lost in history in a man-made myth —
waiting for a call —   waiting.

GRAMMAR

she has no english;
  her lips round / in a moan ....
calligraphy of veins ....
  — MERLINDA BOBIS, 'First Night'

My syntax, tightly-wrought —
  I struggle to let go,
to let go of its formality,
  of my wishbone
desiring juice — its deep marrow,
  muscle, and skin.

The sentence finally pronounced —
  I am greedy for *long drawn-*
out vowels, for consonants that
  desire lust, tissue, grey-cells.
I am hungry for love,
  for pleasure, for flight,

for a story essaying endlessly — words.
  A comma decides to pr[e]oposition
a full-stop ... ellipses pause, to reflect —
  a phrase decides not to reveal
her thoughts after all — ellipses and
  semi-colons are strange bed-fellows.

Calligraphy of veins and words
  require ink, the ink of breath,
of blood — corpuscles speeding
  faster than the loop of serifs ...
the unresolved story of our lives
  in a *fast train without terminals*.

I long only for italicised ellipses ...
  my english is the other, the other
is really english — *she has no english;*
  her lips round / in a moan —
oval, rich, nuanced, grammar-
  drenched, etched letters of glass.

LILY PADS

in the lovely half-light ...
the air was a splendid rose
                    the colour of red mullet ...

tree — had cigarette-paper leaves ....

shells of — sea-urchin ....
— ANDRÉ BRETON

1.

sea-bed
stones —   lily pads,
                        laminated beeswax —
        split atoms
                congeal ions —

2.

... by not wincing one bit
even as bodies fell
                                breath dilates —
starstruck   *starbright* —
left   to calculate
                        equation's high powers —
infinite indices.

i remember the words:
                anatomy is fixed
                        like stars
and *i have become*
        a *still-life on canvas*

3.

a still pond —   lilies —
                pads afloat,

        micro-island leaf-plates,
    buoyant plateaus,   demersal debris.

    water's glazed wedgwood,
            calico glass-veils —
mirror   freezing —
    a one-way refraction's
limitless imaging —
optics   translucent spots, blood-clots

4.

keys tuned —
    black   white
        in equalized variance —
double-tone's elongated vowels
            loop.

a *hope in a piano* —
    hidden in *the cabinet*
        of doctor caligari
    restraining
        the bioscope man —

max saul

5.

in *the garden of earthly delights*
    a beautiful alignment —

the *geometry of taste*
rearranges iron-filings
        to bipolar shapes —

the burnt forehead confounds
    with its headlines
marking time   age

6.

... *by not wincing one bit
even as bodies fell*   just flesh
held by invisible skeletal edge —

like soft shells
gone bodyburst,

like gravel, like photon —
        bursting, riff   bass line —

lines in a will that haunt
        and foretell

7.

it is the seventh note — a seal —
        a memo
              to a person   unaddressed.

ni — ti   in monosyllabic
rhymes —

              scrabble-thrills, seven-tiled
phrase-turns.

"the letter i'm expecting
        is travelling incognito
            in an envelope"
by the 'last post' —

it is my note within a note
to someone —
        perhaps breton —

        perhaps
        abani or *ramlochan.*

indi
pops *hazar* ±   [± dously]
        to mark the exact
              lyric.

sms, g-chats, inter | text —
        linked notation —

        sa — — — — — *ni* | ... *sa*
        do — — — — — *ti* | ... *do*

seven — notes, tones,
                        register scales
like synapse
        arcing — an east-west helix.

sea sand, sonar sand, sun sand,
                        soft shells
gone bodyburst —
                lily pads

৺

AORTA ART

Onion-pink aorta transforms
    crimson-red — tertiary twigs

split, as installation art revolves
    on its axis. They pose

as radiant organic sculptures,
    made even more stunning

by teleradiology's intense probe.
    Five-beat rate scans —

magical images of living organs
    captured remotely

from rural health clinics faraway
    from city's glass-and-steel labs.

Coral-shaped aortas rotate 360°
    in perfect Brownian motion

on vertical hi-res LCD screens —
    scanned images of the diseased.

They are beautiful however —
    illness radiating inner beauty —

hidden architecture, looped,
    dancing in secret helixes.

Teleradiology Centre, Bangalore

MATRIX

Birds fly across the pale blue sky
cross-stitching a matrix in Pali —

a tongue now beautifully classical
like temple-toned Bharatanatyam.

Dialogues in *the other garden*
happen *not just* in *springtime*. Yet

you stare askance *talking poetry*
in silence, an angularity of stance

like a shot in a film-noir narrative
yet to be edited down to a whole.

What is a whole? Is it not a sum
of distilled parts, parts one chooses

to expose carefully like raw stock —
controlling patterns in the red light

of dark, a dark that dutifully dissolves.
There emerges at the end,

nests for imaginative flights to rest,
to weave our own stories braving

winds, currents, and the elements
of disguise. *Fireflies* in *the grove*

do not belong to numbered *generation*[s] —
they only light up because line-breaks

like *varnam* keep purity alive —
enigmatic, disciplined, spontaneous.

Let the birds fly tracing angular paths,
let the dancer dance unbridled,

let the poet write unrestrained —
natural as breathing itself.

Matrix woven can be unwoven —
enjambments like invisible pauses

weave us back into algebraic patterns
that only heart and imagination can.

*She walks porcupines — as you do — and
listens to the sound of the sea in a conch.*

🌱

INNOCENCE
   haiku

  a child teaches us —
to preserve the innocence
  of our small mistakes

GOA HAIKU

1. SHADOW

glittering sea-skin
   at mid-day, shadow-dance on
flint-speckled sand dunes

2. FISHERWOMEN

the oily plaits of
   bronze-toned fisherwomen, curl —
mimicking herring

3. BREAKFAST

diced fresh fruits tumble —
   honey-topped with coconut,
muesli and curd

4. COCKTAIL

margarita glass
   rimmed with salt — stings and blanches —
heat of ocean sun

5. SEASIDE

beach umbrellas, flags,
   towels, table-cloths flutter
with wind's roving tide

6. SHACKS

shacks stacked side-by-side
   heavy with dub-bass trance mix
compete for custom

7. SUN BATHING

topless bodies burn —
    white to flaky ugly brown —
sun scorching secrets

8. SUN BURN

skin smarts, sweats — acrid
    air crackles the deep heat of
the slow salving salt

9. STUDIO

studio's chill cool
    air melts blues — deep blue belies
the red heat outside

10. ENERGY

deceptive slow pace
 subtly streams into my blood —
sparking life from death

TONGUE: DIPTYCH

1. THE VILLAGE, NEW YORK, 1988
for Joseph Brodsky

Not far from your home
   at 44 Morton Street,

our paths would cross
   at a village café —

you made shapes out
   of paper napkins,

yelped out a "meaow" when
   a perfect rhyme was struck.

We would recite
   from memory

epics of yesteryears,
   marvelling at their

lyricism and depth, in poetry's
   pleasure and epiphanies.

With unbridled glee,
   you would twist

cigarette butt-ends
   as if they were calibrating tools

to achieve perfect balance
   in verse's involute tissues.

Late evening sun would cast
   its shadow askance, etching

light's spectral signature
   on our manuscript pages,

as I remembered by heart, words
    from your 'Tsushima Screen':

The perilous yellow sun
    follows with its slant eyes

masts of the shuddered grove
    steaming up to capsize

in the frozen straits of Epiphany.
    February has fewer days

than the other months; therefore,
    it's more cruel than the rest.

2. UTRECHT, THE NETHERLANDS, 2007
    for Mark Strand

Nearly two decades later,
Mark, Jitske and I

remembered you, Joseph,
    variously and fondly —

slipping raw oysters
    down our palette,

sipping thick red wine.
    University's grand hall

saw another epic
    performance —

Strand's honey-slow
    deliberate utterance

marked iambs, making
    the ink on vellum bleed,

blending unlikely tongues —
    Dutch|English, Russian|Bengali —

merging enjambments'
   invisible edges.

It is a matter of tongue —
   how words taste

is shaped by their deft
   muscular curls,

how they let saliva slide
   accents into shape:

Ink runs from the corners
   of my mouth.

There is no happiness like mine.
   I have been eating poetry.

NEW PUBLIC LIBRARY

Nestled within vast air-conditioned glass spaces
    and tiered airport-like transparent corridors,
we are led to the rare-books-manuscript section.

Here I feel the tactility of a book from the 1500s —
    an old colonial gazetteer; even Christ's doctrines.
I caress the crumbling crispness of old uneven

pages, their insect-eaten margins, their faded ink
    that hides and reveals so much at the same time.
Narratives of the past preserved

among hand-written manuscripts,
    carefully wrapped in felt-crimson cloth —
as if the sanctity of the author was at stake.

There is grace and reverence in this simple act —
    a prayer preserved for the soul's afterlife,
a story left unfinished for the scribes to fill in.

Looped elegance of stylized scripts, ascenders
    and descenders etching old classic fonts,
scratched notes on sepia margin spaces —

all these peripherals speak more to me
    than a thousand volumes of clean printed text
bound as unopened-unread-unborrowed books.

A letter falls out from an old poetry manuscript
    I am leafing through by chance.
A lover's letter to her beloved, a star-crossed life

left suspended between despair and hope,
    between longing and uncertainty.
This epistle's last few paragraphs look smudged

with age, time-blurred, as if deliberately defaced
    by the author herself — some memories
are best imagined, left unexplained … in ellipses.

Goa

SAFE

In Room 4, the safe
   embedded in the wall
has not been opened
   in a 150 years.

It has seen history,
   life changing, aging —
but no one knows
   what lies within.

The keyhole looks worn —
   paint-stripped,
pock-marked,
   knife-gouged,

dented scars
   of attempted break-ins
worn openly
   without care.

But what is inside? —
   the first owner's ashes,
her will, wealth, gold; old
   currencies, lover's relics?

Perhaps, it is best
   kept as a mystery
in a world where
   there is so little of it.

A spider runs across
   the safe
weaving silver strands —
   nature strings

her own signs
   of preservation,
of protection — a web
   masking talisman.

Flies buzz around
    marking out
their territory
    in an annoying tenor.

Wall's peeling lime
    flake off, whitewash —
failing to conceal time —
    lose their glue.

A train of ants
    enroute elsewhere
get distracted
    at the keyhole's gape.

Some tunnel in, but
    even after days on end —
I do not see them
    emerge out again.

Gratitude Heritage House,
Pondicherry

RAGHU RAI PHOTOGRAPH

On a river-bank, abandoned clay-idols
of goddesses wait for their last rites.

An old widow clad in a white cotton sari
looks on, awaiting a similar fate.

A cow, half-hidden behind a gigantic tree,
her bovine-head resembling a decapitated

hunting trophy, nailed to the trunk.
Everything is calm — the river rippleless —

a boat plies on, lazily. An emaciated
boatman rests on his long bamboo-oar,

waiting for the meagre wealth clay deities
provide once they dissolve — an ungodly

immersion in the polluted river. Death, life,
ceremony, sacrifice, serenity, ferocity —

frozen meditatively still, find umbrage
under the scant-leafed large old tree.

Kolkata, misted on the horizon
across the river's far edge, looms sprawling —

entirely unaware of a captured drama
waiting to unfold at the city's periphery.

2.
BodyText

I wake up cold, I who
Prospered through dreams of heat
Wake to their residue,
Sweat, and a clinging sheet.
— THOM GUNN, 'The Man with Night Sweats'

You were my death:
you I could hold
when all fell away from me.
— PAUL CELAN, 'You Were My Death'

MAGNETISING DEAD BONES

I am surrounded by tropical green neon — multi-sized screens populated by cursors and graphs whose night jive is determined by every move I make — every cough that escapes my parched throat alters their crest and trough.

It is cold here, very cold. I lie reluctantly on this crisp snow-white sheet, laundered impeccably to create a lasting impression as if it were my last day. Starch has its own curious effect, not just on your so-called gait, but also on the sleep-cells.

The colour of this room is blue, endless blue that seems almost black. Against this, the radiated glow of green and its tiny electronic letters and numbers, the nurse-white linen, the stale starch scent — all trying their best to induce a lullaby. However, this languorous soporific lyric is making me feel colder, rather than the warmth it is supposed to inject in me.

Injectables can be dodgy these days; you never know their ultimate intention or point. A prick here or there is hardly going to change my blood chemistry at this age — but to dull my senses, it works.

A figure enters my room. I can make out only the person's shapely, starched silhouette — her curves complemented by sharp lines and points, almost bearing a geometric sense that resembles a hastily planned post-war burial site.

I am cold and getting only colder. The bones in my body are freezing to such a brittle point that even mere breathing might make them snap. Waveringly, I can hear my corrugated breath too, clear as coarse air in a tunnel, its velocity summoning up its strength as the forces build up. I like the sound of air rushing around, it has a sense of assurance about it, never predictable, and always there even when everything else disappoints. I like the fact that I have the power to create air, sculpt its shape, direct it channel it and even consume it.

The person in the room can sense the electricity, invisible photons lighting up this intimately controlled space. The transfer of magnetism between us, with its latent live power, would be dangerous at this stage — both of us know that. So it is best to leave our hands untarnished, even though all the heaving circulations map an intensely charged field that leave even the iron filings in complete disarray.

I distractedly try to speak, forgetting for a while that my voice box has lost all its essentials. Only strained echoey sounds, like the ones in my imagined air tunnel, emanate. The hoarse timbre matching the searing edge of steel that is to graft my skin shortly.

It is quite odd yet strangely warming to imagine the sound waves that a crystalline rock would create when one carves out lines on the face of volcanic granite, to form a newly emerging poem. Metal, rock, text — all ingratiatingly severe — would satisfy my urge, an urge to get out of this sanitized capsule — a capsule where the range of colours is as broad as blue, black, blue and black — their heat extremely chilling, icy.

Suddenly, one of the screens sparks, creating a flurry of beautiful short-lived streaks. Post-mortem reveals a short circuit, the result is heaps and heaps of ash — tangled electric ash — powdered bone ash. Ash is meant to be very good, sacred, and virile in its content.

Now this is the stuff of dreams — a semi-darkened space barely lit by the colour of molten green; soft grey dust in abundance for me to blow around, to control the airspace by marking out my new patterns with trained ash travelling through still air. Contours would have to be remeasured, terrain to be remapped.

All I need is my breath and breathing strength, and my imagination. But I lack the former. I assumed that they would be naturally present. But one does not account for decay, least of all when your mind is buzzing. They say imagination can conquer anything, even the body. It isn't true.

My body now has a hollow feeling running through it as if all the bones have been stripped out, leaving only the intangible flesh to find its shape. As long as I am harnessed to the electrodes, connected to its current, the shape will be retained artificially to deceive the onlooker. As long as there is no power failure, I can present myself amicably. But that may not be for long. That is why I feel a great sense of urgency to create while there is some voltage left. In any case, what else can I do? — Nothing really, certainly nothing that is worth any effort.

At least here I have been granted a mound of ash, a palette of blood, syringes that ooze metal, uncut crystals, electrolysed bones, and clean white sheets. I feel grateful to possess all these. At least I can begin where memory began, start the early sketches and the bare-bone drafts of my metred text. The lyrics, if they are meant to, will emerge at the vanishing point.

WISHBONES, ARIAS, MEMORIES

There is enough left in my bones that every morning is an undesired struggle. I wake up weighed down by a burdensome dilemma of what to do, what to construct for the next twenty-four hours. My mind seems annoyingly alert, but I feel sick, exponentially sick — body and soul dissipating, though not as fast as I would like.

I have long craved some kind of a resolution, but such kindnesses elude me. My heart still sends just enough oxygen to fuel the think tank. It stays artificially active, in fact overactive, enough for a normal person to be electrocuted. Unfortunately there are enough fire extinguishers in sight to quell such quick exits. My bones, muscles, fluids are all deliberately drying up. I feel their creak, their fading music, and their lack of will — there is such beauty in all that.

As a regimen of forced distractions, I try reading but the letters blur as soon as a sentence seems to form. I watch television and everything on it appears monochromatic and visionless. I walk but I have no destination in mind. I work but I have no ambition left. I write my coded pieces, but no one takes any notice of the hints.

I feel trapped in my own body. The cosmetics of appearance defy their very truths. My skin belies the reality of my own health. The science of survival battles against my intentions. But there is such dignity in this opera. Only an aria waits, patiently like an unformed Buddha, hoarding all my truths.

My bones still support me, even though they are brittle and fragile as hollow columns of ash, charred long before they were polished white. They soothe whatever is left of my senses. They allow me to imagine shapes, architectural structures balanced in space — free space where tariff and gravity seem absent and redundant.

I find myself in a toyshop, the only adult among children. They look at me, sneer at my grown-up state, except now I am more child-like than they are. I came here looking for bones, not bones from the dead, but plastic ones, ones that allow a child to learn the building blocks of life, to construct and set up a model for their life, to feel the tactility of life itself.

But plastic bones do not have the satisfying chill and grit of real ones. Yet how can I confess I came looking for real bones. Perhaps I should donate mine, all two hundred and six of them, so that someone else like me who comes along later to look for the same does not have similar difficulties of shyness and honesty.

What is the point of constructing the text of an epitaph when your very own family wouldn't care to read it? How can one expect others to consume one's writings? That would be sheer indulgence, wouldn't it?

But grave cravings have no formal logic. Such mathematical sequences are mere flights of philosophy. No wonder even the earliest grammarians equated genius with madness. Mismatched spaces are comforting to me but not to anyone else. Order is sanity. I have no space in such charted constitutional narratives.

Real lies swim deviously in shallow waters. The more still the surface, the more electric and jarring its current. But hollow bones have an uncanny knack of altering the current charts — alternating between sane and insane, insane and more insane, sadness and more sadness, directness and indirectness. My bones may have some purpose after all — their calcium could turn poisonous, and the poison may finally allow me to see the possible worth of the next twenty hours. I need some poison every morning. I could even grave-dig to find poison.

For the moment, that remains a mere hope, as I begin to doze off — into a dream. There, I travel variously in a tenuous red and white vessel made of tissues. The tug and steer guide me to a calcified cavern as I negotiate the terrain — splintered shards of bone that look like stalagmites and stalactites compete to meet each other, their jaggedness trying to pierce all my invisible pain, perhaps to jump-start my memory that once had the safety of poetry stored in it.

Memory is at a premium now, so are words. I would be immensely grateful if someone would help finish my poem 'Approaching Death' more swiftly. There is grace in such actions. Grace is what I most admire and trust these days.

FEVER PITCH

The seductiveness of a slim tall transparent glass tube — the curved silver juices it contains — is such that it makes me forget the news of the birth of a new child. Human life and inert chemical life compete in insidious ways, the same way fact and fiction do, as do desire and disgust, illness and passion.

Like an aria, it is a curious melody, as distinct from harmony — a solo part in a cantata or opera. Its inherent nobility and splendour, its treble and bass create an enigma of its own private architecture.

The mercury in the thermometer rises, gradually and numerically, to a height where human equilibrium can just about balance itself. I stand at its base. The glass chamber rising many storeys above me holds a reservoir of finely granulated liquid that changes its silvery-grey shade in the fading light. Above that, a constriction, then a towering shot of fine tubular glass hoping to reach a degree of sanity at the cost of human heat.

Summer is already approaching outside; my body sweats gently in appreciation. The heat worn by my skin's surface is nowhere near the heat that is slowly welling up inside me. It takes the lightest of touches, a feather-swivel for it to shoot up the scale. But, at the moment, all is calm as the storm gathers pace.

I am dying for the monsoon rains — but I am caught. Trapped in the wrong longitudes, these wet dreams are dreams that will have to remain un-soaked. The hair on the surface of my skin itches to raise its hood to attract any pheromone in sight. There is a magnetic lull and hush, a loud silent sound of breathing, in different voices.

Platoons of clouds clash softly without any hint of thunder. There are electrical impulses that are waiting, poised to spark. But the perfect noiseless moment is what everyone is waiting for. Only the obtuseness of instrumentation can clarify that, but that would be too intrusive.

The mercury shows its first sign of life — a little trickle, then a tremor, then a surreptitious U-turn past the erectile crystal-tissue. Thereafter, complete freedom. It is at this point that the human's heartstrings and the chemical's soul marry perfectly. Each follows the other's actions, responding on a natural impulse, like the soothing scratchy sound of ice severely eroding under a ballerina's silver skates. Metal matches metal, breath matches breath, glass matches ice, freezing the heat itself.

I sit — serenely delirious — on the convex tip of the mercury's crest. All around me is vacuum — and beyond that glass — and beyond that a semblance of life and world. Here the vagaries of temperature do not seem to matter — a sanitized skyscraper holding the elements of inertia and energy. Here I feel particularly buoyant, not because of anti-gravity, but at the hint of rising temperature.

This is the third thermometer I have bought in a day, and yet I cannot trust it. Twice before, the reading shot out beyond the graduated scale itself, hinting either I was heated to the point of insanity or it was a case of the glass's own neutral impotence.

This time I am determined to get to the heart of it, inside its very core, whatever the consequence. However, when one is caught in the process of creating a grand score, it does not matter what the root causes are. Genesis, like the Christian one, should remain a Buddhist mystery — then all religions can command the private power of the elements themselves.

Molten silver — boiled, cooled, boiled, cooled, boiled, then caressed variously over skin — finds an intimate space that intersects the point of heat — glows, dense and quiet. One knows the gravity of such events, but not their intimacy, not their relationship with follicles that create their own forest fires with their own human climatic changes.

It is these alterations that marry physics, chemistry, biology and mathematics — there is hope in all these — just like the sine curve's elasticity and predictability, the graph's nodes are stretched straight on the X-axis, the subjects collude to a point of nullity. At the point of birth, there is the death of the womb itself, but one lives — so there may be hope.

It is at such interstices that art and passion find their true shape. The unknown boiling and freezing points that I hide within myself provide the ultimate enigma that even the most specialized doctors and architects find hard to map. My body is a terrain that defies the contour of safe plotting — indices like Celsius, Fahrenheit, torque are all inadequate — just as bone marrow count, triglyceride, HDL, LDL do not form pretty, explainable equations.

Amid this oratorio, the cold tactility of a three-faced glass case, its triadic ancient constancy, its contained columned virility, provides comfort to my talisman. Sometimes even the most brittle seems to find some soft shape for hope. Silicates form so many forms — but what I like most is their stubborn transparency, their supine pirouettes, like the vicissitudes of mercury — like breathing itself — at least until they last.

HEAVY WATER

There is something deeply arthritic about water and pain, the way water seeps into unexpected fissures in bones, the way it conducts pain itself — operatically, electrically.

This morning I woke up, as I usually do, in pain. It was a new sort of pain, a pain that I had not encountered before, so I didn't know how immediately to respond or manage it. All this while, I had sorted and filed each type of pain into neat bearable files, each with their possible recourse to relief, albeit temporary.

It had rained all night, and this morning it continued without any relief. The sound of persistent rain once provided calm — but all this water sound, with its chaotic decibel, was annoying my breathing, heartbeat and sight.

Whether my sight was blurring due to water battering my retina's windscreen or whether it was triggered by the slow accumulation of pain in my heart was difficult to measure or analyse. Only intensity and volume mattered — cubic litres, millilitres — almost any equation with letters and numbers raised to the power of three. Triadic superscripts — n^3 — there lay some oblique clues, but perhaps only to the initiated or those who wished to be part of its intimacy.

The irony of intimacy is such that the closest in the family seem the furthest away. Their attempt to be interested, in spite of being uninterested, ultimately measures pain and its intensity. Intensity is a peculiar thing — its measurements are tactile and ephemeral, quantifiable and infinite. It is measurable, its heat and depth fathomable.

It is the ephemeral that is painful. Water creates all the confusion — its saltiness, its acridity, its mineralized purity, all compete in ways that chemical equations find hard to support or balance.

Families of electrons, protons and neutrons speed away, whirring in patterned loops, forgetting all the while that the heart of their orbit may actually feel and breathe. But in science, as in the ambitious ruthless route of success, there is no room for unscientific thought — as if science and the arts, coolness and emotionality were mutually incompatible or different from each other.

I am in pain, and I just want to cry, cry and cry — so that each searing cry can etch some fragment of a note, which has gone unnoticed, so that each measure of pain is no longer diluted for people who listen because they have to.

I wish to paint a canvas that invents new indices of pain and water, for anyone who wishes to listen and bear, for anyone who wishes to understand — not because they need to, sitting comfortably straitjacketed — but because they are moved by it. We need to be moved, moved by the finer chords of music and art, so that both electricity and opera can operate as they always did, in tandem.

But heavy heart, like heavy water, is difficult to dissolve — their melting and boiling points register unusual scales — scales that peal and peel, echo and layer, untying each and every fibre that breath requires in order to survive.

🦂

'O' ZONE

The spray of scented chill pierces my lungs first, then comes the slow desperate heaving, the grinding spasm splaying, trying to centrifuge stubborn coves of mucous — whose greenish-yellow viscosity remains more deceptive than quicksand's subtle death trap.

My face — confined in the transparency of plastic, frosted glass and thin air — regains for a moment the normalcy of breathing. It is a brief magical world. The oxygen in my blood is in short supply. I feel each and every electron's charge, spurring my senses.

Dizzy in aerosol hope, I try to free myself of the medicated mask, but the frozen rain that batters my face reminds me of the tentativeness of living. As I survive on borrowed air, I'm grateful to the equation of science, its man-made safety, its curious balance that adds that precious molecule to create the sanctity of 'O_3' — the holy Brahmanical triad — and the triumph of its peculiar numeric subscript.

My breathing is temporarily back now — electrolysed, perfectly pitched and nebulized — as narrow transparent tubes feed dreams into my wide opaque palate.

The sun's edges are dark, so are my heart's. No amount of air will light them up.

NIGHT WARD

The night ward's blue curtains that surround me drip colour and deceit — each and every pleated flute of cloth hiding some half-truths like the half-lives of atoms. Only here, the arithmetic surety of fission does not wish to match the nuclear chemistry of my blood's transfusion.

The night nurse peeps in to assure me that blue is not all black, that red is not grey, that the colour of my skin does not reflect the colour of my life. I wish I could agree with her consolations.

Yards of white and blue linen that wrap my slow generous chill, know the real secret of my floating corpuscles — the flotsam larvae, their ancient silk that gently threads my nearly finished mummy.

❧

ICICLES

Cold blast from an electric vent bites my skin — this comfortable discomfort, prickling my pores bathed in an acrid glaze, transforms to frozen gold-salt.

Attaining instant freezing points might be a rare marvel of science; I like this hellishly good blast that shakes all the embedded molecules in my bones —

bones that are parched in heat, turn to skeletal icicles — a beautiful ballerina-geography of stalactites and stalagmites — each needle-end points towards the other

like the two longing fingertips in Michelangelo's painting at the Sistine Chapel — desiring a touch.

PHOTONS, GRAPHITE, BLOOD

There is a lamp — blue and white enamelled — that hangs straight down from my room's heaven-white concrete. The electric noose balances the bulb's epi-centre directly above my desk. The conical curvature of the shade's inner wall contracts every electron in sight. It is well made and hardy and cheap.

I had picked it up at a random flea-market sale. It lay innocuously next to a stack of old seventies blues records and a box containing pins, clips, angles, lead, string, bandages and pieces of magnet. Curiously, this lampshade beckoned to be rescued from this potpourri of discards. Something about its shape had attracted me — its mathematical precision, its nonchalance, its latent heat and its misplaced future.

A few weeks later it found a place of pride in my studio. It became my invisible body, a talkative metaphor making up for all the uncomfortably annoying silence in this space. It took over my space, colonized it, and then started writing my pieces for me.

It had been dark for many days. I didn't know whether I had lost my sight, or if it was one of those infamous marathon Delhi power cuts, or whether the act was waiting for a curtain call before the next show. There was no show, or if there was, it was for an audience that failed to show up.

I got used to this darkness. I even started liking it. There is something wonderfully warm and safe about the dark. It allows you to hide, it allows you to rant, it allows to you weep, and it allows you to die unnoticed and emerge as another person — if you are lucky — without anyone else realizing that an intense metamorphosis has taken place.

Another night — I had returned from the outside to the dark safety of my small space. There was a glow, a light that I had always imagined but failed to see, or perhaps always seen but failed to notice. But it was the next act, the unwritten stanza that altered the entire narrative.

A pool of light lay splashed on my desk. Its circular cast shimmering thoughtfully on the page where my poem was arrested in mid-flight. At its periphery, the circumference began to fade, inaccurately. Even the power of pulse and wattage showed their fragility when one of many flies buzzing on this sweaty night sat on the metal shade. Then everything changed.

There was another power outage, a major one, but that was normal in the country's capital at this time of the year. However, this lampshade remained magically lit in full flight. Its rays billowed out as if it had caught the right trade winds on an unnamed sea. There were no generators or invertors to assist this 'load-shedding' — I can safely assure you of that. It was as if my blue and white conical companion had mysteriously extracted all the electricity in sight, condensed it into the tiniest invisible atomic space, and then, like escaping blood, let it ooze out gently, as it would after an accidental pinprick.

The blood spread, surreptitiously approaching the lone fly that had by now flown from the lampshade's edge on to the tabletop. It sensed war; flexing its winged muscles, it prepared to take the right stance, so there would be minimal bloodshed.

The light's heat and intensity made the fly forget its natural act of flight. It started moving, centipede-like, towards the approaching lava. The blood trickle changed tracks, carefully avoiding an unwanted spill, not smudging my metaphors or the neatly constructed lines. The fly chose to use the moment of enjambment at the end of stanza three as its vantage point. The bloodstream, sensing the birth of a new metaphor, stopped in its tracks, allowed itself to gather into a bulbous expanding sphere of crimson, and then using the overhead light's strength, gathered speed, training its path between line spaces, dextrously dodging images that protested its progress.

I had used handwritten italics as my script. The trail my HB pencil left, calculated the latitudes and longitudes of the paper space very carefully, unknown even to me. Amid the dark doldrums of this papier-mâché seascape, the unscripted theatre seamlessly enacted itself.

Suddenly my eyes distractedly went to the last unfinished line. There I saw a dead fly, frozen still amid the glass-ruins of a burst electric bulb, splattered with blood, and the shattered lead's shimmering graphite. I also saw lines that I had not written — imprinted in my own script, planted on the page. The poem was suddenly alive, screaming, weeping, nervous, calm.

I looked up and saw a new bulb. A red bulb had replaced the vanished one in the lampshade. The shade's colour had altered dramatically to a rusty metallic — almost like stale blood. The pool of light had permanently frozen on the page. And there was also a poem — an unannounced gift of hidden light.

RURAL MAPPINGS

Morning unfolds very early in Ahmedabad's Dhanasuthar Pole — too early even for the sun's clear sight. The clatter of unwashed utensils on the streets, prayer call from the Swaminarayan Temple next door, the loud repetitive groans of cows being milked — all this and the sounds of a medieval town preparing itself for the waking of dawn.

I lie in bed, awake much earlier than I would normally be. It was a fitful night. I plotted an imaginary graph all night, mapping the ancient stars on this room's ceiling — a ceiling that has been held up for two hundred years by uneven lengths of tree trunks, whose flaked bark and skin lent resilience and resin — all put together tentatively, to hold the weight of the constellation of small heavens.

A body lies next to mine. It is warm — warm in body heat, quilted cotton, breath, and tropical air. Her eyes are closed, but not entirely shut — a suggestion of sight keeps her pulse in hunt.

I touch her skin. A little twitch records my finger's roving imprint and its wide caress-tipped arcs. Her face is perfumed with the fragrance of feminine sleep, her breath with the grace of a swan's wing sweep. She is treading water in slow motion. The ripples she draws and redraws are unnoticeable, except to the most intimate eye.

I watch her breathe. Her eyes record the intensity of shielded gaze. It is a dream, a dream that is possible only in a half-awakened state — a state where skin, blood, saliva and heartbeat are exposed to its essential bare. Bare like my over-exposed receptivity, bare like a sparrow's under-skin, bare like the god's skin-polish in the temple's sanctum sanctorum.

This god's body has been caressed for hundreds of years — mornings, evenings, nights, and all times in between. It is relentless, all this religion and fervour of touch. It is not even private touch, but a sea of fingers continually seeking to satisfy their own want. And so, the polish. Polish of invasion, polish of desecration, polish of passion, polish of peace. But this is god's duty and place — and there is something immovable about it.

All of a sudden, a band strikes up. Its raw uncoordinated notes fly around like torn pieces of old newspaper from a garbage van gone astray — the print indelible, the notes not yet scored. We have no choice in altering the text or the narrative of cacophony that beat upon us.

Not just me, even the gods want to retreat. But there is no place to do so. It is believed that the law of old towns and their scriptures demand that one must endure — endure patiently — whatever it may be and however long it may take.

POSTCARDS

For decades, I have received postcards with an annoying sense of regularity. They have arrived from all possible places — from a burnt-out garage warehouse where a Beat poet friend and I once shared an echoey studio space; from the hop-stained boiler room of an English pub's brewery; from subterranean 'larger-than-life' 'sewer-pipe-dwellers', who ever so often would surface to leave bits of text for the groundlings. I got one postcard even from god, but most of them came from hell. The last pile gave me most comfort, understandably. But amid all that, I had to carry a perennial burden, an unwanted guilt, for not having replied to any one of them.

Choicelessly, I have preserved these postcards with a sense of undisclosed fervour. It is quite unlike the one that grips you when you numismatically collect copper–nickel disc-change, or mint-condition serrated quadrilaterals in search of philately. And all these come with their inherent quest for value and nationality, their insistent obsession for identity and status — 'permanent resident', 'resident alien', or the 'other'. Residence and permanence have little meaning for me, only the postcards with their unexpected origins, their marginality, their addresslessness, provide safety to my kind.

On the obverse six-by-four papier mâché space of laminated gloss, my created cast of characters variously enact themselves — Milo, Yacoub, Madelaine; Anna, Alexandra, Zoe; my lost brother Jake and many others. Their postures pose truths and [un]truths that ultimately make sense, even if, to only a few.

Cards arrive from the remotest corners of the planet — from a half-restored fifteenth-century mansion, 'Gartincaber' in Doune, lost in the Scottish wilds; from a moss-ridden ancestral house, 'Chandradham' in Bankura, soaked in rural Bengal as its age-brittle bricks try hard to keep the plaster and lineage cemented; from an invisible deckhand on an abandoned rust-ridden ship run aground on Bombay's Bandra shores, a cinema set 'Goldmist' balcony in the frame without Basu-da's presence — all these and much more, constructed by fate, reason and madness.

Madness is the only space I can inhabit, the only space left for me that makes complete sense. I am not allowed to do anything else — my hands have long been severed by the executioner, my bank account robbed clean by my employers, and my blood caught in a corpuscle-thickening dance that unwinds itself in deliberate movements — slow and artful.

And all along my alter ego constructs buildings of fantastical proportions — made of titanium, gossamer and glass — their skeleton held together by enjambments and line breaks that defy even geometry and gravity. I trapeze along — sketch with the likes of Wright, Kahn and Corbusier. I find it astonishing that I remain unelectrocuted, having balanced my laser-linear space on the death-torque steel of high-tension wires. I spin ferociously, heading towards the fountainhead, where the topography of the atlas shrugged off its dead weight and epicentre. I want to be an architect, and a map-maker.

Every morning I wake up to the peculiar and unmistakable 'brass-and-wood' sound of the postman sliding insidious parcels through the letter box — epistles, epigrams, epigraphs; lyrics, lust, latex; cantos, cantilevers, cadavers — all scored in perfect pantoums and set in arranged arias in a lattice-looped typeface.

But I am not awake, I mean really awake. The diurnal time distrusts me — weighing me down under the albatross-noose of a day job, the persistent fetid tones of telephone calls, the distressing iambs of food shopping, dishwashing, and keeping the mortgage-till in order. The day passes, unremarkably. Then it is evening and soon night-time. Now I am awake, certainly much more fully.

I go through the rituals — gurgle my throat with the black ink of chilled stout, wash my mouth with vodka laced with more vodka, followed by a smooth stream of single malt — and slowly, very slowly, I reach a plateau, deftly suspended in gentle equilibrium.

My mind, now, perfectly poised to kill any distracted gerund in sight or snap up any misplaced metaphor loitering around. Nothing can stop me, not even the fangs of the contorted walrus-toothed Everyman — that desultory Smirnoff copywriter — who rewrote the very definition of 'spirit level' itself. Heaney would be happy. So would Brodsky, Walcott, Neruda and Paz; as well as the entire distilling tribe.

An invisible song erupts. I see myself in an old church. A swan-graced cellist with the electric beauty of pale youth swims in to steady the waves. Her angelic brows dip, as the long lamentation of her deep-oaked cello breathes, resuscitating the congregated air with secret notes, notes that strangely escaped from my hidden postcards. I hoarded them all these years not knowing their implications or their desires. Now they bloom, magical and perfectly intoned.

I run to the temple. There is no faith left in the apse — only the memory of slender fingers stroking the cello, Chandipath's baritone invoking the myth of Durga's verse, and images of italicized scribbles.

It is morning again — time to retire. I put my night gods to sleep. Another postcard threatens to arrive through the door's letter-vent. I am grateful for such meagre company.

But all of a sudden — I am apyretic, apyrous and aqua-cool — I am not at all my own self. It is merely the beginning. I can scent a bloodstained epistle on its way.

3.
VARIATIONS ON WAKA
STILLS FROM SANSKRITI

... rising fogs prevail upon the day.
— JOHN DRYDEN, *Mac Flecknoe [I]*

The ... fog that rubs its back upon the windowpanes.
— T. S. ELIOT, *Love Song of J. Alfred Prufrock*

Stills from Sanskriti

TRIPTYCH
three haiku

❧

STAR GLASS

    tiny-star-flecked grass —
scattered mirrors cut-pasted
    to reflect the sky —

❧

LEAF ON WATER

    slate-edged lotus pond —
mosaic-leaves fanning water
    bloom, refract white light —

❧

ARCH

    red sandstone arches —
gateway to beyond, through which
    everything passes —

NOTE: This poem-sequence using the classical Japanese waka-form was initially written as a site-specific piece of creative work mapping the geographical terrain of Mr O P Jain's Sanskriti Foundation on the outskirts of Delhi. The overall production will include collaborative work by British artists — Jenny Lewis and Frances Kiernan — involving innovative theatre, composed original music, art, collographs, book sculpture, experimental photography, digital video projection, and performance.

MUSTARD
tanka

Mustard blooms swaying
under the sharp winter sun —
shed pollen — yellow

rain. Banyan tree hides butter
cups for Krishna — Radha waits.

BARAHKHAMBA
haiku

a lone teak rises
in the square of 'twelve pillars' —
uncapped, free-spirit

QUARTET
four katauta

CENTRE

the wild beds around
Barahkhamba and Banyan —
flowers for your room centre

❧

GAON

in Gaon's courtyard,
a *tulsi* sapling — in the
village centre, sacred tree —

❧

IRIS

red-eye and iris
focus, sight locking axis —
diagonals dove-tail light —

❧

SHAPE

silhouette, a form —
artist alone centre stage
poet alone studio space

AMALTAS
choka

   Broken pillars lie
defeated, scattered around

   aimlessly in mud —
different lengths retelling

   different stories.
Huddled in a heap amid

   a weathered concrete
grave, Amaltas germinates
bringing life to the ruins.

🌱

HAVELI
bussokusekika

   yellow jasmine floats
on still water — an *urli*.
a Buddha-like head
disengaged from its body
sits patiently at tree's feet —
petals, grass, path, haveli.

🌱

INSTALLATION
sedoka

   seven marble slates
large, rectangular, cut white —
leaning as three triangles
   anchored tight, live-earthed —
another on top, like a
table-top, lifeless, brooding —

4.
LADAKH

In a land where it seldom rains,
a river is as precious as gold.
— ALICE ALBINIA, *Empires of the Indus: The Story of a River*

the mountains, and the aridity.
a formless jumble .... form a system of parallels ....
— JANET RIZVI, *Ladakh: Crossroads of High Asia*

... colourful flags flutter above the boundless
heart of the river.
— ZHANG ER, *Verses on Birds*

ZOJI LA PASS

                at 12,000 feet
slopes steeply.   Hard snow
                cut into two
by winding tarmac —
                a severe cold-slice
freezing to a stand-still.

❧

A car meanders
            through this open-air tunnel —
ice walls on either side —
                a geometric strait
                      resisting
the warmth of diesel's grey metal.

❧

Two yaks on the lower slopes
                look up for colour
in this blinding white.
Their horns storing clues,
                      anticipating
the mood
                of changing temperatures.

❧

In this rarefied air
                    lungs shrink —
breathtaking breathlessness —
                clarified oxygen is sparse here —
high-tone octane echo in the stark terrain.

DRYPOINT PLATES

Slants, slides and slopes
                of striated mud-screens —
barren altitude's blank-plate burr —

not white — just shades of brown,
          dark brown, light brown, camel.

The air swirls endlessly
          kicking up
                  cylinders of dust columns.

Soldiers guard this unforgiving landscape
          standing firm in their allegiance,
mouths covered in black combat-veil,
                skin ruddy in uv light.

The road here is broken gravel,
          slate's splintered edges
soft-land on dust and more dust.

An angular slate slice —
          catapulted by a passing truck's
hot tyres
               is flung high,
spinning in a blur,
cutting the air in a slant.
It skeet traps
          a clay-pigeon's path —
shot down by wind-currents
                bulleting the windscreen.

Glass cracks — pin-point minutiae —
                        web-streaks
fan outward in recklessness.

Dust and mud and sand,
              desert's drypoint print —
its softness belies
              the powdered hostility.

ZANSKAR-INDUS VALLEY

*Every wave is filled with rubies, water perfumed with musk,
from the river waft airs of ambergris.*
— SHAH ABDUL LATIF (1689-1752)

a foul and perplexing river.
— LIEUTENANT JOHN WOOD (February 9, 1836)

Valley's green carpet
                      punctured deliriously —
fruit trees, grain, crop —
          the Indus soft-washes all.

This is mere infancy —
          the mighty river's
new journey, born
upstream
     in Himalaya's
                   snow-fed spring.

Swimming steadily —
          civilization maps
ancient cities,
        Harappa's
manicured waterways
and Mohenjo-daro's
               perfect grid,
ravages of war
          and blessings of silt —

the river floods — fusses, dances dry,
          then resuscitates its alluvial skin,
and diva-like
     immerses gloriously,
disappearing   in the Arabian Sea.

Under the Indian Ocean
          the river remembers its birth —
a birth that I had witnessed,
     its nascent waterfall anointing
                   my palms
as I, in slow motion, drunk from it.

KARGIL

Our street of smoke and fences, gutters gorged
with weed and reeking, scorching iron grooves //
of rusted galvanise, a dialect forged
from burning asphalt, and a sky that moves //
with thunderhead cumuli grumbling with rain, ...
— DEREK WALCOTT, *Tiepolo's Hound,* Book One, (II).1

Ten years on, I came searching for
                war signs of the past
expecting remnants — magazine debris,
unexploded shells,
      shrapnels
               that mark bomb wounds.

I came looking for
                      ghosts —
people past, skeletons charred,
abandoned
            brick-wood-cement
                that once housed them.

I could only find whispers —
                whispers among the clamour
of a small town outpost
                    in full throttle —
everyday chores
            sketching outward signs
        of normalcy and life.

In that bustle
          I spot war-lines of a decade ago —
though the storylines
        are kept buried, wrapped
in old newsprint.

There is order amid uneasiness —
                the muezzin's cry,
the monk's chant —
        baritones
        merging in their separateness.

At the bus station
               black coughs of exhaust
smoke-screen everything.
                          The roads meet
and after the crossroad ritual
                               diverge,
skating along the undotted lines
                                 of control.
A porous garland
               with cracked beads
adorns Tiger Hill.
                     Beyond the mountains
                             are dark memories,
and beyond them
               no one knows,
                             and beyond them
no one wants to know.

Even the flight of birds
                       that wing over their crests
don't know which feathers to down.
                     Chameleon-like
they fly, tracing perfect parabolas.

I look up
       and calculate their exact arc
and find instead,   a flawed theorem.

DRASS

At "world's second coldest
                inhabited town" —
early signs   of change.
            Kashmir's
walnut   wood-
            work,
                    serif hand-script,
willow glowing in linseed oil

            gradually give way —

Leh-wards —

                    to monastic metrics,
graphics,
        a predominance of
                            white
        highlighting sharply
the definiteness
        of primaries —
red, yellow, blue | red, green, violet —
            clothed in
        masonry, mud, linen and silk.

Cylindrical wheels
        rotate from left to right —
palm-prints, prayer, and paint
                            mix.

                Radiant forms —
holy   right-angled
doors, window's
        stepped edges
                spawning squares,
        slow-shaping
the omnipresent   flutters.

MAGNETIC HILL

Anti-gravity
        halts cars in transparent

      white boxes, boxes
that do not appear
          to appease
              the magnet seekers.

     The long tarmac,
          its black and coal
mimics
      lode iron,
             attracting filings.

The road is edged —
              dust and mud-sand
inch their way in gradually
            changing reversely
the tar's matt to gloss.

Magnet's levels of attraction
              turn distraction
      into unbalanced axioms —
fulcrum shifts
        as does weight,
class of levers,   and axes.

GOMPA

    Wine-red robes,
                  sash-cloth belts,
    hold religion
        body-wrapped.

    Against white
                mud-washed
    gompa walls,
        coloured flecks
    of cloth, texture their face —

    looped fonts
               in matt-black —
    imprint RGB, CMYK
        on white, cotton and silk.

    Flattened oval stones
        eroded by devotion

    keep perfect time
               as time sits on
    top of each other
        balancing the granite greys
    in ascending order.

    Scattered clumps of
                chortens hand-built
    as markers,
        markers
    keeping eternal heartbeat
                blood-pumped —
    breathing
        spartan abstinence.

CHANT

om ma ni padme hum

blank contains
        everything —

everything contains
        nothing —

nothing contains
           all.

all is one —

        one is many —

many is all.

om ma ni padme hum

INDUS

Indus

        [H]*indus*

[S]*indus*

        Ind[*us*]ia

↕

        Ind[*us*]ia

[S]*indus*

        [H]*indus*

Indus

PRAYER FLAG *(reprise)*

Prayer flags
               flutter —

I try to catch
          their flight —

their song, their words,
their flap.

They are quiet
          in their colours —

the colour of river,
snow,
          earth, leaves, sun.

They are waves
          that turn the earth,

the earth moves them.

Five colours implode —
        mix,
then   white.

SNOW STRUCK

1.

A tiny tent,   a pyramid —
    red nylon
        gripped on metal lengths
heated a huddle inside —
           human breath
was the only warmth
      at 15,000 feet.

2.

That night the wet swept
        the cover's taut skin —
as I heard rains rustle,
    wind swallowing
          frozen half-chants
wafting from a gompa close by.

3.

Yesterday,
    I had sighted a couple of monks
        at this remote height,
their squint-pupil gaze inviting
        prayer's glimpse, its mystery.

4.

At night though,
      sleep-awake through
an unexpected snowstorm,
      I felt the frailness of fragility
and nature's oblique ways of healing.

5.

In the morning, I tunnelled out
        through long-zipped door-flaps
to a welcome —
        beautiful blinding snow,
                fresh, powdery,
and a dzo's fierce stare.

The herd's white-washed   marsh
        anchored their black definition
and their rough breath,
their arc-horns turning
        like subtle radar-swing —
the slightest invisible tilt
        possible only in this still rare air,
captured
        chilled on damp canvas.

6.

A lone young monk called out "jullay"
        inviting me for yak-milk tea —
its thick translucent taste
        stoked my giddy breath
at this unsteady height.

I saw a flight of menacing snow-clouds
                approaching,
        but now I knew
how to embrace them.

PRAYER FLAG

Om Ma Ni Padme Hum
O the Jewel in the Lotus
— Inscription on a Tibetan prayer flag

1. MANAS SAROVAR, MOUNT KAILASH

Frayed, flapping in the high winds —
    prayer flags gently unravel —
homage to the day's first light.

But today the dawn is not as bright —
    heavy, brooding, silver-grey
like the lake's shimmering glass-top.

No one is here, except for a woman
    staring far away,
wrapped in the sanctity

of continuous linen — her own sari
    like a prayer flag —
though devoid of any colour.

She isn't mourning or crying,
    just gazing fixedly
into the water's changing glimmer,

as the sky's wet weight
    and the shore's rocky line meet,
their edges meanderingly

melting into the lake itself.
    I stood far behind her,
behind everything she saw.

2. PRAYER FLAGS

She was only
    an accidental figure
in the wide-screen frame.

Unlike her,
    I was looking skywards,
through the prayer flag's

translucent cotton,
    counting each thread
of each piece of cloth

that wove private stories,
    whispered *only* to me.
Weather-worn, strung across

canted multiple horizons,
    I tried to map
their own geographies —

each an island,
    each with its own terrain, texture,
inscription, and scripture.

Found on the highest points
    on land, as close to the sky
as is possible,

these magic carpets —
    shapes caught on
an unintentional clothes-line —

were more meaningful to me
    than this vast
monastic scenery.

How each flag — each one,
    must have preserved secrets
that *only* their owners knew.

How each, a talisman —
    exuded safety and calm —
shrouding away grief

for the briefest while,
    when one forgets everything —
real, imagined — and just dreams.

3. PILGRIMAGE

My own piece of cloth
   that I'd once tied onto this line,
wasn't visible to me now.

But that did not matter.
   I found strength in this
procession of private passion,

in these flags' lack of starch
   or hierarchy.
Their stories passed down

by one flag to another,
   toggled hand in hand
through time and age —

just like my pet yellow butterfly
   who infused each flower
in my garden with the gift of life

without any show or fare. I like
   the transparent quiet here — I also
like the wind's occasional sound,

its severe current tearing through
   the flag's heart — picking out
the perfect pitch and melody.

4. BUDDHA IN A LOTUS

A memory now, a still — framed,
   not revealing to the world
what I had once seen —

the panorama's generosity,
   its wild, stark untouchability.
How each story

stitched and preserved
   like the jewel in the lotus —
its crystal-fine edges

caressed by petal's soft skin —
    until,
everything folds inward —

like a foetus in a womb,
    a toppled misplaced comma,
my own implanted memory.

And then, they bloom,
    fanning outward —
each flag, strand, story,

each private grief and pleasure —
    chanting noiselessly
in the mountain's silent winds.

[inspired, in part, by a photograph by Deb Mukharji]

5.
RAIN

In the lap of the storm clouds — the rain comes —
Its hair loosened, its sari borders flying!
— RABINDRANATH TAGORE

At the end of this sentence, rain will begin.
— DEREK WALCOTT

RAIN, MAPS

It has started raining — sharp shards of transparent sheets hit the glass of the window that threatens to crack, but upon meeting its surface, melt to water. There is a constant blur of water outside. It is a curiously inviting scene, one that seems misty with flickering crystals glowing in parallel striations — the patterns changing their tack depending on the wind's mood-swings.

I look at this grand show of rain everyday and everyday I weave a different pattern, both due to my own mood and the weather's inherent currents. Each day I weave a little piece, adding a patchwork to this infinite quilt, one that buries unwanted narratives in the warmth and cosy of its apparent comfort.

The way the quilt's colour and imprint form is unpredictable. The only thing that is known is the exact square-inch space that each segment will add up to. Its individual design is unknown until it is stitched onto the larger stretch of linen. It is a journey, mapping a route that is largely undecided, perhaps even unknown.

I like this mystery. It allows one to completely imagine and plot a path that suits one's own sense of direction. I have a compass to find the Earth's cardinal points. But this is of no use when it comes to details of terrain, temperature, vegetation, and the inhospitability of travel itself.

I like the unknown, the unpredictable, the sense of encountering the virgin, even though the path might have been traversed before. But I do not have that knowledge, so it is entirely fresh, untrammelled, and personal. I begin walking.

I can walk anywhere from almost anywhere. I do not need time-tables, or ports of embarkation and disembarkation. I do not need guidance of the tourist trade, or the help of someone who has done it before. I just venture out; let my legs do the walking, my eyes do the seeing, and my heart do the navigating. And amid all this, my mind keeps me company, as I imagine, dream, and see — visual and virtual, spontaneous and sure.

RAIN, RAIN

It is another space, another view, but the same rain. It has been raining all of last night through to this morning. It changed to a drizzle for about twenty minutes before resuming its full fury. But in its fury, there is an overbearing sense of surety and steadiness of intention. There is a constancy with which the water pelts down the striated streams of liquid.

It is hot and muggy, though clear — one of those slow languorous days, deceptive because it looks hopeful and bright at the outset, but the moment one attempts to do anything, it starts raining and a heavy soporific lull sets in.

🌱

LANGUOR, WET

A typical start to a Kolkata day, more like an extension of last evening. The quality of light is the same as yesterday's — deep grey with an immense cloud over-hang. The electric lights inside are still on, as though they weren't turned off last night. There is a heavy, brooding, damp quality in the air that seems to invisibly wrap my exposed skin. My hair feels humid — even the upholstery, the clothes, and the trapped house-air.

I step out into the back garden. The soil is clayish and waterlogged. The plants look prosperous and overgrown though the lack of sunshine today does not highlight the clarity of fresh green. The insects, caterpillars, and spiders are busily getting on with their business, entirely unperturbed.

Rashid, our guard and gardener, sits outside under the drive's front-porch pondering what to do. He has a perennial uninterested look that transforms to a semi-bright spark whenever any of his employers are in sight. There is a lot he could do, but he does very little, blaming his inactivity on the weather.

FERN FROST

In front of my desk, the glass-panes on the window are frosted — but the temperature inside is not freezing. Outside, the tropical pre-rain humid-heat of the afternoon makes the sight of broad-leafed palm trees, an epitome of brooding languor, and plenitude.

The air in my study is cool, perhaps even conditioned cold, relative to the heat outside. Plain acts of physics and geometry make simple sights alter their guise; change from one state to another, even though that may be transitory.

There are definite mathematical equations to corroborate such sights, well-tested algorithms — but for me, illusions provide more room for imagination than the exact state of space.

The palm-leaves outside are huge, enormous like large fern-sails, their edges defined by the crisp 'cut-n-stitch' along their invisible seams. Their strength and dignity must come from the elegance of their trained spine.

All this is much like the gaze of a sophisticated onlooker — a visualiser — who sees the same scene with a different sense of calm, poise, thought, and imagination.

AIR-CONDITIONER, RAIN

Isolated amid air-conditioned comfort, vast well-cleaned concrete spaces, and the shelter of tropical profusion, I feel completely cut off from the hustle and bustle of metropolitan living that I have been used to for decades.

It is cold in this room. The temperature belies the climate of the external topography and terrain. It is this chill that keeps me awake, otherwise the dull humidity of outside's dead heat induces an infectious sleep.

It is raining again, but today's is a beautiful kind of rain — steady, symmetrical, confident, and unobtrusive. It has a kind of presence that is omnipresent without actually announcing that it is there, like 'ambient' music, though that would be too cruel a comparison. Somehow technological similes used to compare elements in nature are always fraught with dubious results.

I work here having lost the sense of time and its own presence of metre. Somehow natural syllabics have their own quiet momentum, one that leads you forward, setting their own pace and mapping their own space, much like the process of breathing itself.

Natural breath pace and its pauses have always been crucial to my own sense of textual pacing, the way they wind and twist displaying its curious unpredictable intentions.

HEAVY METAL

Ship-breakers, snake-like in a single-file, slither towards monumental vessels stuck aground in the rain-swept muddy delta. This is Chittagong's heavy-metal graveyard, where abandoned big queens of the high-seas are left to reminisce about their past glamour and glory.

Most of these workers are day-labourers — each, like a foot-soldier in an ant march, is an emaciated cog in the giant flesh-and-metal machinery — most of them untrained in dismantling thick sheets of steel. Their mud-coloured bodies glisten, as their gleaming sweat and the acrid-water's viscous reflection in the marsh-pool threaten to boil-over in the sun.

But there is hope — hope for a colony of people earning a temporary meagre living — hope for the virgin-soil — to mingle with the poisoned rust of the ships so that both can learn the effect of contamination — and hope too for an onlooker for images that propel creativity.

The ships stand, rain-soaked, statuesque in spite of their exposed dismantled skeletons. Bit by bit, they will be further broken down and sold for scrap metal, and many of their fixtures will be sold as display-items in brass and antique shops in the big cities.

Scrap metal never held such fascination and beauty in my eyes before. In spite of this wet panorama's unconventional composition — the scene somehow had a haunting quality of expansiveness that defied the obvious imagery of labour, extortion, and death.

MONSOON GREENS

Green is the colour most visible to me these days — glazed-oil green, light-banana green, olive green, dry green — the green myopia of politicians; the green armoury of warfare, the green undergrowth — all twisted and weed-like, green and unstable, and no one in sight to prune or train them.

Shades of verdure have caused a blinding effect on my system. Trendy herbalists are wrong — instead of a soothing, calming effect, green has a peculiarly vulnerable, nausea-inducing effect on me.

Green bile and vomit, a Frankenstein-fantasia, green-mucous cough spat by tuberculosis patients, green moss and grime in unclean toilets and storm-drain ditches that line the roads — beautiful green, awful green, healthy green, wet green, monsoon green.

Monsoon has arrived — persistent in intent, green in jealousy. The rain is going to be around for a while, only hastening and never dampening the insidious, monochromatic, chameleon-spread of green itself.

༃

BENGAL RAIN

Rain has sparked so many imaginations all over the world. But there is nothing like the rain in the two Bengals — West Bengal in India, and Bangladesh.

Rain in its overbearing gait, its preparation, its stature, its brooding quality, and its romantic heavy-lidded cloud structure. Ordinarily one would call these rain clouds 'cumulonimbus', but that name or model does not in any way do them justice.

Here the clouds assume a deep-grey-black quality, and just prior to a heavy downpour it is almost pitch-dark. The leaves rustle around in little circular flurries, there is a pregnant heaviness in the air, the smell of wet clay and the hustling sounds of birds taking shelter permeate the sky.

Barsha, as the monsoon rains are locally known, has a truly unmatchable resonance — elegant, weighty, ponderous, raw, but always striking and graceful.

RAIN CHARM

Another rain swept day leaves everything water-logged — ponds, drains, streets, and rivers — everywhere water is overflowing. The green blades of grass in the garden lie submerged under a rippling shallow sheet of water. Through refraction, they take on magical underwater seaweed shapes. Except here, the grass is evenly cropped, so it appears as a glazed woven mat of wet-green. Rain has also left the plants and trees gleaming, bursting in plenitude.

Natural irrigation in excess creates its own slow-rot, a sublime slime of wet decay and birth, profusion and irresistibility. Rain has this special seductive appeal — its innocuous wet, its piercing strength, its gentle drizzle-caresses, its ability to douse and arouse. The entire charm lies in its simplicity.

❧

NIGHT RAIN

I woke up at 3AM with a start. I was shivering and sweating profusely at the same time. The cotton T-shirt I had on was completely drenched. So was the bed-sheet I was lying on.

Outside I could hear the rain hitting the terrace floor with relentless ferocity. Thunder-claps shook the glass panes to near breaking point.

I love the sound of water and rain whatever their mood. It has a certain sense of assurance, a steadiness that isn't always present in the other elements.

I had a spontaneous desire to step out into the rain. I was drenched anyway, so getting the rain's feel on my back would do me no harm. Besides, getting wet in the night rain has its peculiar thrills.

I stepped out — my body heat met the rain. The rain-water sizzled off my skin steaming up in curls of white vapour.

All I could see and imagine was a blanket of hoar-frost that enveloped me and the rain. Night rain camouflaged in the steam of body heat.

SHOWER, WAKE

The September showers came too late, giving ample time for a prolonged drought. But when they eventually arrived, they brought with them the full fury of an unstoppered monsoon — the rain pelting down hard, cracking open newly laid tarmac, exposing the earth and the elements once again.

The pouring water persisted, overflowing until everything was affected — weak roofs, power lines, trees, un-warned shelters, people — almost everything.

After two weeks, the storm subsided — a war-struck wet wake lay shattered in the aftermath, hungry, heavy, and low like polluted clouds of mist over a submerged *mofussil* that was trying to breathe and periscope back to life.

But here, the arteries are severed too severely to recoup its strength anytime soon. With or without water, in flood or drought, the existence here remains unchanged.

༃

DROUGHT, CLOUD

It is bone-dry — I pray for any moisture that might fall from the emaciated skies —

There is a cloud, just a solitary cloud wafting perilously —

But it is too far in the distance for any real hope — for rain.

༃

KNOWLEDGE, NEED

"The more you know, the less you need" — but that is not true at all for thirst, water, or rain.

6.
EroText:
SIXTEEN MOVEMENTS ON EROTICA

*I want
to do with you what spring does with the cherry trees.*
— PABLO NERUDA, 'XIV: Every Day You Play....'

Sex is need but Eros is desire.
— ROLLO MAY, Existential Psychologist

INDIAN DESSERT

Clumps of wet-smoke simmer in the pan, and slowly
    lift to caress the outline of your breasts

as you cook, stirring spices in carrot, milk,
    and cream — ingredients that conjure

recipes of hunger and passion. As you melt
    sugar and butter and gently stroke

flakes of grated almond-shavings,
    more clumps of perfumed smoke permeate through

the silk of your shirt — now transparent in heat —
    painting the outer circle of the nipples

to a hardened edge, tasting the sweet
    skin, the surface of the crinkled base,

to a creamed mouthful of untampered delicacy.

❧

DESIRE

Under the soft translucent linen,
    the ridges around your nipples

harden at the thought of my tongue.
    You — lying inverted like the letter 'c' —

arch yourself deliberately
    wanting the warm press of my lips,

it's wet to coat the skin
    that is bristling, burning,

breaking into sweats of desire —
    sweet juices of imagination.

But in fact, I haven't even touched
    you. At least, not yet.

ABSENCES

Our mattress is the wide ocean,
    the crushed sheets, the waves.
We sail together, full blown.

But during your long absences
    as our ships are docked
on different shores, sometimes

the bed dreams — I imagine, the wet
    breaking the anchor loose, defying
gravity, current, and electricity,

as photons propel and burn
    even the wild salted expanse
into a monument, a desire,

permanent like the ocean bed,
    its pulses uncontrollably rocking —
the waters, the bodies, the dreams.

❧

TASTE

    Our skin
breathes love

    through
its pores,

    the glands
transforming

    shivers
into taste.

    The taste
of desire

    is the taste
of its warm

    lingering
after-taste.

❦

LYING BARE

Your bare stomach
    is my pillow.

When I turn
    my head

on one side,
    warm air rises

from the valley
    to lull me —

on the other
    side,

you shield my sight
    of your face

with your bosom —
    to devour me

in the gorge
    near your heart.

MORNING

    Buried in warm skin
toasted in the night's passion,

I struggle this morning, to emerge
    out of this heavy air.

DAY BEFORE SUMMER SOLSTICE

We are sealed in marriage today
    to celebrate
tomorrow — the earth's longest day.

We are mere stardust of an ancient
    supernova — one that gave
us our metal, blood, and breath.

KISS

a languorous kiss —
    the faintest smell of ocean —
salt-lipped breeze, pleading —

SKETCH

Pencil-strokes
    that ultimately

end
    in inked lines

has a woman's passion
    for a man.

Small things
    matter — eyebrows,

wrists, and
    gentle demeanour.

CLIMAX

    Lips
of a rose-

    bud
open,

    to let,
the dew

    drop
in.

🌱

RELEASE

The stamen
    raises

its head,
    bursting,

to shed
    pollen —

relief-rain
    showers

the parched
    folds

of
    pink skin.

🌱

LONGING

The very last drop of rain
perched on the edge

of her navel —
the last bead of sweat

balanced on the feather
of her eye-lash —

the last long-wet
of my kiss on her skin —

all these demand more,
more, more —

more wet, more wet —
yearning for more rain,

fire, desire, moisture —
and the cool chill of

crystal-water, thirst,
saliva, longing, rain.

❧

GLUED

together, we lie
   incurably conjoined.
Just as the sky
   and the earth are joined

by an indeterminate
   horizon, so are we, made
one by an indeterminate
   faith.

❧

AFTER SUNDAY BREAKFAST

The morning-scents of your half-awake
 body, bristle at their pores

scampering for fresh places to hide.
 They run furiously toward me — across

the stitches of the linen-draped table,
 carelessly dodging milk and juices.

Pheromone intoxicated, I stagger
 floating in the sparse early sunlight —

your fog-filtered apparition —
 warm skin, that comes to life

boiling in pumped blood —
 effortlessly moulting a rebirth

like yesterday's left-over croissants
 just heated, very crisp to taste.

WANT

Summer's
 dead heat —
humidity
 teasing clouds
to shed rain —

absolute
 stillness —
every leaf
 balanced,
tentative,

eager,
 quivering,
aching to feel
 the moisture
on their skin.

RAIN

The heavy sediment of fine espresso sinks — in a deliberate silent slow-motion thud — to the bottom of my glass mug. My head is infused in swirling aromatic fumes that wrap the morning's fresh-green rains. Moisture's deep taste defies my body's intention to stay dry.

It is cloudy — deep grey and about-to-burst — they over-hang teasingly, arching their backs, pregnant with wet's many-prismed face — merely seconds short of relief.

Everything around is still dry, though the damp's constant warning makes me wait — tentative, unsure when the cloud-burst will release all its heat.

But imagining the rains can be far better than relentless rain itself. At least, one can control its intensity of downpour, wind, force — imagine its desire, definition, and direction.

🌿

7.
Wo | Man

Images of your face
Bring me
The wild mane of summer leaves ...
— BEN OKRI, 'A Gentle Requiem'

the soft tumult of thy hair
— JAMES JOYCE

HEATHER

I lie next to the sea. It is dead still, except for the invisible rippling soundless undulations the water makes as it breathes. There is no moonlight, but it is not pitch dark.

You kiss me everywhere — everywhere, for hours and hours and hours. My lips are dry, my body salt-encrusted. You have eaten every bit of pleasure, yours and mine. I feel parched, dry, in spite of all the plenitude of water and our sweat.

The sand too is sweating beneath us. Every grain remembers every wave, every caress, leaving behind just salt, a silver layer of salt as a gift — a talisman of love, of their inconsistent meetings.

I feel parched like the sea-salt gauze. My tongue is parched in spite of your lavender saliva, saliva which has changed from that bouquet to the taste of heather, wild weather-ravaged heather.

I look around for light, but I can only see reflection. There is more beauty in second-hand glaze — the sky's dark light radiating off your lashes, the water's blue light hiding in your navel, the beach's grainy light lying unwiped on your nipples, and the light's invisible inner light stored in your pupils.

The sea is getting restless. But I am dead still, except for the inaudible swishing that I can hear when you press yourself against my heart.

I need to taste the grainy light that you wrap your skin in, each and every grain that maps the slow deliberate contours of your body.

FEMININE MUSK

1.

My body temperature is steaming, higher than the highest calibration on the thermometer stem. I need to get out of this hot house.

I go out, walk past the stream, to the overgrown meadows. There is a lake at the end of it. I am not a swimmer — but I like water on my skin.

Blindly, I follow the foot-worn mud track to the shores of the lake. It is a very large lake that almost looks like the sea. This stretch is isolated, visited only by people who might stray from their course.

I reach the water's edge. I dip my feet in it. It is freezing even on what I thought was a hot scorching day. Maybe I am misguided by my own body temperature.

I unbutton and take off my sweat-drenched shirt. My jeans are drenched too. I cup my hands and scoop out palmfuls of water and splash it all over me. I am drenched, seemingly cooler, but still hot in heat.

I let my feet dip in the water and lie back on the shore's wet mud. I do not know when I doze off — lying dead still.

2.

The taste of cold glass in my mouth wakes my senses. A cross-country trekker who happened to pass by this route thought that I must be 'not-quite-dead' but close. She decided to stop, take out the medical kit from her rucksack and help me.

When I open my eyes, my sight is a little bleary. I can't quite focus, but I see an outline of a woman's face, her hair falling all over my face and her naked chest as she kneels over me, holding my hand, counting the pulse beats.

I am not quite there yet. She takes the thermometer out of my mouth, reads it, and then without saying a word takes her scarf off and dips it in the lake water. She puts the drenched musk-cloth on my forehead, pressing down gently, letting the cool water wet my hair and upper body.

I do not say a word; how can I — I think I am dreaming. She does not say a word. I just look at her, long and silently, hoping she does not think I am staring at her.

She is wearing well-worn ankle-high Birkenstocks, denim shorts, a skin-coloured sleeveless vest, silver stud earrings and a silver necklace with a stone pendant that dangles very close to my lips. Her kohl-lined Wedgwood-blue eyes have a deep penetrating gaze.

Her wet scarf on my forehead is trying to bring my temperature down. But my body heat is rising. I can only smell the air's heat, my body heat, her heat, her female scent — I am feverish and woman-soaked.

❧

CAROLE

A white flower — desire — . . . In the night. What the insomniac [like me] saw . . . In the snow, a fire alphabet. Huddled there.

Carole Maso's Aureole drips passion on to my lap. It is too much to hold it there. I fantasize, salivate — fantasize about Sappho, Carson, Winterson; about the ancient Tamil poets who wrote about love and lust, the erotic and the spiritual, with equal fervour — no hierarchy, no shame, just celebration, pure instinct, pure blood, pure ice.

Their text plays havoc with my mind — electrocuting my body — their metaphors too hard to restrain, their passion infinite. I get lost, delirious with words that paint filigree screens on camisoles that aren't transparent or opaque, visible only to those who read Braille.

Writing on skin, on paper, on pillows, on bedsheets, on stone, on wood, on metal — there are no constraints, no medium that is unsuitable, not even water. Only my mind edits, and nothing else can. I can destroy words physically, ban them, burn books, but I can never erase the narrative and poetry from memory. Words — our greatest gift, our only strength. It is a tactile act, writing. Writing paints. It dreams, it weeps.

My wordsmith is a miniature painter, a quiet artist. She is an incessant lover, she is obsessive, she is relentless. She is kind, she is gentle, she is feminine, she is exquisite. She resides in the 'Exquisite Hour', she lives in Maso. It is magical, it is intoxicating:

The slur of your touch. Her eyes glacial blue. The opium of your touch . . . You suck on the stamen of a poppy. More contented — oh yes . . . Ashen bridegroom in white . . . Magic.

GOLD SQUARES ON MUSLIN

1.

I admire her crisp off-white muslin — it is sheer and full of well-worn elegance. It has — spread sparsely over its cotton — scatters of delicate little squares of gold, zari woven by hand, intricately, with care, two generations ago.

These little pieces of gold spark narratives — revealing intimate secrets of family, motherhood and friendship — stories hitherto hidden in a silo, secured steadfastly within the hierarchy of starch, grace and poise.

But this sari is also wrapped around someone whose body is not quite there. Invisibly present and distracted, she remarks to me —

'Look at the clock, it is so late.'

2.

The clock shows different times on the same dial — reminiscing two separate moments on two separate continents, simultaneously. The same time is two different times for the two of us. And yet we are part of the same story.

The slender hands move with mechanical precision, not mapping the irregular heart and pulse beats that burn constantly inside my body. The clock hands appear to move fast, or not at all — and that is the fate of our histories.

3.

Outside, I can hear the breeze gathering force over the waves as the tides prepare for the evening, their crests rising higher and higher. They make insistent surf noises, as each crown of white foam releases a strong scent of seaweed and salt. This is enough to make me intoxicated.

Inside, I sit on a white-cushioned cane sofa to catch my breath. On a side table next to me stands a large white porcelain lamp with a wide-brimmed off-white lampshade. On its perfectly convex belly are characters in bright red, painted and glazed in Oriental script.

So much is hidden in so little a space — a flourish of a Zen-like haiku, compressing more than it reveals, providing calm in such turbulence. The Japanese characters mean 'happiness' in Kanji, and that quietly uplifts me more than my friend can ever imagine.

A clear low-watt bulb hidden behind the lampshade casts a circular spread of light on the heavy teak of the floor — the illuminated space and its fuzzy-edged circumference merges with the yellow of the light and dark brown of the hundred-and-fifty-year-old teak.

4.

The sea breeze enters the apartment with its heady scent. The lemon washed walls, the white ceiling, the books, the glass and granite banisters, the surety of wood, and all the bric-a-brac from the world over provide the mise en scène of a film that has never been shot.

Yet all the characters in the cast are ready with their well-rehearsed lines, poised to trip off their lips in perfectly intoned delivery. I, too, am on the play's cast — a very minor character — a mute one — my tongue slashed for speaking of the heart's peculiarities.

And yet, I do not know any other way to live or to act — I just have to act the way my spinal split-ends direct me. Only in this unmade film, the master puppeteer's many strings carefully hide the excruciating pain that I carry permanently on my bare back's nerve endings.

5.

My friend tells me that we all have to mark our lives with tattoos of comradeship. Invisible tattoos they may be, but they have to be etched all the same, in spite of the pain that accompanies.

So, we summon the best tattooist in town. She is an artist with the slenderest of fingers, and nails that reveal under them parallel striations of blood that give colour to the unpolished surfaces. She is a miniature painter and has the most exquisite hand for understated design. Her eyes have a sharp-honed focus that is so intense, that it can, in a moment of instant combustion, split white light into its seven strands.

Amid all this, I can only provide her with translucent white ink, one that she mixes with earthy natural hues. And the rest spontaneously draws itself out — exquisite, with an elaborate concentration of detail, minute and passionate.

6.

I can hear voices, other people's voices — movements, shifting of paper.

'The demons constantly hover around in my mind,' my friend said. 'And now they are talking aloud, making themselves heard'.

All this pain, a whisperingly silent pain, in my bloodstream — this shingle-sharp pain seems to reside permanently in me.

7.

Next evening, on Mumbai's waterfront, I sit dangling my feet over the embankment with the sea below and Gateway of India behind me. I swallow the brackish air once again, taking in deep gulps. They provide brief toxic relief to my broken heart.

The brilliant evening light that, not too long ago, illuminated the sandblasted ochre face of the monument and the white boats on the blue-grey seascape, has now faded. In the descending dark, the sea smell tries to induce a misplaced sense of romanticism in me. Selfishly, I try to grab on to any illusion of love that comes my way, but my heart can only gather the heavy weight of gloom.

8.

I start making my way back to the friend's apartment that I now call home in this city. It is perched high on the city's skyline, watching over the electric night canvas of the streets and buildings below. I hope that upon my return, all that glitter and the sea scent will lift my spirits.

I, so dearly, look forward to those little gold squares on the muslin where I want to paint pictures. I want to talk to the little girl in my friend's small blue and yellow painting that has her fighting the winds to keep her umbrella in shape. I want to reread the poem that is inscribed below it.

But upon my return I see that the muslin canvas I longed for has now vanished. It has been replaced with ordinary black linen, a colour I have dreaded facing, a colour I had donned myself last night.

9.

'I hope we have at least gathered strength from our comradeship,' I tell her upon my arrival.

'Our desire for love, for death, for rains, for chemical smells of paint, for Edith Piaf,' I said, 'is all meaningless, without our desire to breathe fully the air we create, and are inherently blessed with'.

'Let us go then, you and I / When the evening is spread out against the sky . . .' — *'Chool tar kobekar andhokar Bidishar nisha . . .'* — Damn it, why do I only remember other people's poetry, poets whose work I admire, old lyrics, sad songs? — All this memory, there is too much latent memory.

But then, why not — you are an old companion — and I have been writing letters to you on onion-skin paper that I bought in your city. The paper has traces of lavender petals embedded in its pulp; its pages are bound in purple leather with Devanagari script printed on it in gold.

But this is not the gold I desire.

10.

I still search for the off-white muslin to write and paint on. But it is too far now. I can see it in the distance — it is now a sail on a fishing boat fast receding into the horizon.

And the recent brilliantly orange-red sunset is stunning for the same reason as the level of toxins in my bloodstream.

'Wear that sari again,' I ask my friend. But she can no longer find it.

WHITE

1.

It is evening. The soft, half-warm orange glow of the setting sun skims off the sea-skin into a high-rise apartment, lending its white walls an amber colour. Two friends, Banalata and Timur, sit talking endlessly, sipping 'writer's tea' — the Japanese pottery the tea swirls and nestles in lends its own oblique infusion. White cushions on cane chairs, dark wooden floors defying white, a white painting with a red receding heart, a white lamp with red letters imprinted on its off-white ceramic.

As all these construct their own parallel narratives, I glide, straddling a pair of large bird wings, swooping over the rust-coloured sea. In the same apartment where the wall's canvas has been temporarily transformed, Banalata and Timur continue talking, unaware of me outside their picture window. I come flying here from hundreds of miles away, from the north of the country, every evening to hear the stories — stories of love, of grief, of laughter, of friendship.

I have my own friend too, the one that allows me to fly, the one that lets me sit on her soft back as my limbs clutch at her breast, allowing me to hear her heartbeat.

2.

One of the tea drinkers — Banalata — dreamt of me last night: I was sitting in a stark white room that contained only a piano and nothing else. No, there was something else — two beautiful female forms. I was taking photographs of the two young women who were wearing white — just white, white on white, white without white. One of them wore a wide-brimmed hat with white felt trimmings. The other wore platinum-white anklets.

Banalata kept calling out my name, but I was unaware of her voice — I couldn't hear any sound except for the shutter-click of my camera and the whisper of the swishing fabric of the women's costumes. I continued with my work, unaware of anyone's voice. I could only see the two bodies gliding into different positions, like water does, shaping itself in transparent white containers.

Banalata said it was bizarre — I thought the transposed dream was even more bizarre. Somewhere the black-and-white negatives were altered or misplaced or incorrectly washed. The image was white.

3.

On a candlelit stage in the city, I see three friends reciting poetry. Two of them are wearing black — one of them has a distinctive long red crumpled-cotton scarf draped around his neck; and the third in the centre, white. The centre-white sings exquisitely, moving seamlessly from mantra to azan to raga, moving in and out of words — words in Urdu that make even the minutest skin-hair stand on their ends, words in English that make prayer flags in the Himalayas flutter with the gentlest delicacy, words that make silence sing, words that remain quiet, words that resonate from my friend's throat in understated marble-white.

4.

Banalata visits a hospital in her city, as I do in mine. One is crowded, the other empty.

I like empty hospitals. I love their stark eerie spaces filled with instruments that deal with disease and death. I like the white beds, the whiteness of mummy-wraps, the whiteness of cotton and gauze. How beautiful it is when blood stains the white, and the red imprints its dominant strokes, scarring the white stillness.

For now though, everything is white — white walls, white floors, white lights, white tiles, white gloves, white coats and the white of paleness.

5.

The red calligraphy on the white lamp in Banalata's apartment must have been done in the artist's blood. That is the only reason its lustre still glows deep crimson in the white light.

I know the calligrapher well. He handwrote my first book of poems two decades ago. I had promised him a poem in return for his art. But for all the time since then, I have been unable to write. All my poems remain in my head.

6.

Today after so many years, I wrote one for him — a poem, etched on white handmade paper, written in white ink. But I know he will not be able to decipher this colour — neither the transparency of white, nor the white's opacity. But in his mind's eye, he will sense its essence — and that is all that really matters.

My text appears only in white — it will remain white — its narrative invisible to all, and visible only to a few.

7.

White is holding her colours close to her chest — the rainbow struggling to escape from her cleavage refracts swiftly back to white. The big white bird is witness to this, so are the white candles on stage, the sheer white chiffon on the two women, the white parchment, the white ink and the white of the white light.

🌱

BLUE

    Deep dry turquoise of the sun-drenched
Nicaraguan skies are sucked clean

    by the infinite azure — the blue
of your dress, blue of your hair-band,

    the light-blue leather of your sandals,
of the lake's unsure shifting skin, and

    the Egyptian emerald-blue stone
crowning an antique silver ring

    that you recently slipped around
your slender married fingers.

    So much blue should blind vision
with happiness. But this colour belies

    an outward stir — calm that agitates
silence into words, Arabic font styled

    in slanted serifs, hand-written
from right to left, cadenced, your nose pin

    subtly reflecting the glittering phrases
hidden in your practiced letters — beautiful

    lines, lipped, crystal-kissed, smoke-stained,
lisping, failing to hide a deep bipolar love.

SILENCE

Silence has its own
    subtle colour.
Between each breath

pause, heat simmers
    latent saliva —
tongue-entwined lisp.

Here and there,
    errant clouds wait,
yearning for rain.

Desire melting
    even silence to words —
word's colour bleed

incarnadine, as your lips
    whisper softly
the secrets of your silence.

Your fine *chikan* blouse —
    white, sheer,
and almost transparent —

cannot hide the quiet
    of your heart-beat
on your wheat-olive skin.

The milk-white flower
    adorning your hair,
sheds a solitary petal,

just one. In that petal
    silence blooms colour —
white, transparent white —

    pure white silence.

MOHINIYATTAM

Like coconut palms bent,
   swaying in the ocean breeze,

you twist, turn, bend
   sinuously at your waist, torso —

solar plexus balancing
   posture, passion, art, divinity.

Mohini, the enchantress
   embodies — *lasya,* grace —

soft and languorous,
   adorning *sringara,* the beauty.

Your pupils' eye-line extend —
   your brows stretch, doe-eyed —

the *kohl*'s exaggerated arc
   amplifying the deep desirous gaze.

Your sari's milk-white cream,
   silk and gold, melt —

the borders merging,
   yet distinct.

Fresh jasmine crowned,
   angled on the left, askance,

radiates raven-black shine
   of your coiffure, each hair-strand

reflecting gold's noble aura,
   ancient lore and love.

Yet you wear this
   with simplicity and grace,

bear lightly
   the tradition's heavy age.

It is finally the *lasya* —
   mohini's ultimate gift,

the enchantress' longing —
   elegant, beautiful magic.

BHARATANATYAM DANCER

Spaces in the electric air divide themselves
    in circular rhythms, as the slender
grace of your arms and bell-tied ankles
    describe a geometric topography, real, cosmic,
    one that once reverberated continually in
a prescribed courtyard of an ancient temple

in South India. As your eyelids flit and flirt, and
    match the subtle *abhinaya* in a flutter
of eye-lashes, the pupils create an
    unusual focus, sight only ciliary muscles
    blessed and cloaked in celestial *kaajal*
could possibly enact.

The raw brightness of *kanjeevaram* silk, of
    your breath, and the nobility of antique silver
adorns you and your dance, reminding us of
    the treasure chest that is only
    half-exposed, disclosed just enough, barely —
for art in its purest form never reveals all.

Even after the arc-lights have long faded,
    the audience, now invisible, has stayed over.
Here, I can still see your pirouettes, frozen
    as time-lapse exposures, feel
    the murmuring shadow of an accompanist's
intricate *raag* in this theatre of darkness,

a darkness where oblique memories of my
    quiet Kalakshetra days filter,
matching your very own of another time,
    where darkness itself is sleeping light,
    light that merges, reshapes, and ignites,
dancing delicately in the half-light.

But it is this sacred darkness that endures,
    melting light with desire, desire that simmers
and sparks the radiance of your
    quiet femininity, as the female dancer
    now illuminates everything visible: clear,
poetic, passionate, and ice-pure.

NOTE: The line-end rhyme-scheme — *a b a c c a ... d b d e e d ... f b f g g f ...* — maps and mirrors the actual classical dance step-pattern and beat — *ta dhin ta thaye thaye ta*. Left-hand margin indentations match the same scheme and form.

ODISSI

It is her eyes, her wide-open eyes, her large kohl-lined eyes — I sit mesmerized. More than the electric buzz on stage, the arc lights' angled shafts, the strict lyricism of music and its metre, the silk-silver swirl of costume, and her fluid posture — it is the pure abhinaya that stuns me into silence.

I adore Kali, I adore Parvati, I adore Madhavi, I adore the trance-like temple postures — so pure that the stone art of the ancient Oriya temples melts to human form, exquisitely carved, yet breathing, breathing with the passion only reserved for the gods. And yet she is human, touchable.

I can only trace imaginary lines with my human hands on the stage's black canvas, trace the ever-shifting female form, her heaving breathlessness that matches the subtlest half-taals and bols.

Architectural love and body love are one for me — my love for stone and love for the female body are one and the same. There are no hierarchies for me — if temple art is elevated, the dancer's art is sublime; if idols are timeless, the dancer is immortal — but she lives,

lives through my passion as long as passion lives in my body, one that is quiveringly linked to every movement on stage — as her soft alta-stained feet meet the wood of the stage floor, as her mesmeric narratives caress my imagination, as her liquid gaze sculpts every passion to perfection.

Petals, incense, anklets — pallavi, moksha, ashtapadi — her pleated silk sari stores secrets within its folds — jasmine in her hair and on her slender wrists, antique silver, her fragrance, her skin scent, her eyelashes, her lips, her curves that sculpt shapes — it is magic — crystal magic that transforms ordinary into celestial, celestial into mortal — resuscitating even the dead, infusing life, infusing passion, creating dreams.

I continue my imaginary sketch on the black backdrop, its invisible form guided only by the cadence of human breath, her breath — her breath that is subtly matched by my own. Stone and flesh are one, silk and sweat are one, heart and head are one, female and male are one, one is one, she is one.

ALMOST A TOUCH

kodanda rama, gambhira rama —
ranadhira rama, mamadhira rama —

Moving ever-so gently, diagonally towards each other,
    your lower torsos draped in off-white linen
bear delicate crimson-green borders of matted gold.

Your outstretched hands, the two dancers' finger-tips
    about to meet, but instead you change tracks
to move in a parallel line, and then in a smooth circle.

You depict the story of Ram's bow — *kodanda*,
    of the strict line of periphery — *Lakshman rekha*
breached — its dangers of trespass and longing;

of Sita's disrobing — undignified, shameful unwrapping —
    valkalavastra — a mere bark protecting devotion;
stones the monkey-platoons gathered to form a form.

Bamboo, bark, earth, rock — elements that construct
    wave-like arcs, arched snake-hood, the fangs, the tips
always seem to touch each other but do not —

stopping just before the nail-tips feather-touch.
    Looking into each other's eyes — directly and askance
your feet mark another map, a map that love defies.

You swan-swim with a dancer bearing my name,
    your upper torsos bare and open like your hearts —
deep-felt nerve-ends — electricity waiting to spark.

DEDICATION

1.

Soft as water
    you tread the ground
touching every tiny part of your feet's under-skin —

        heel-ball-toe —
as if your need to leave an imprint of your step,
    to befriend the shifting earth,
is urgent, entire and whole —

2.

Then I spot you in the fading light

on the peripheral dirt road of Sanskriti
        where I walk everyday —
    your movement
like a *tai chi* artist approaching
    a seamless shape —

3.

Your desire — to move, to explore,
        to connect as a child —
was unmatched by your filial military alignments.

Instead martial arts
turned to skating
        forming beautiful figures,
fingers tracing arcs to make art
        on paper made of rice,
calligraphy in wild cursives.

It was as if breath was passing
    through your entire body,

pulse by pulse,
        each molecule deliberate and wanting,
                wanting to map
and make history travel through your skin,
melting as it passed along —

It was an exploration of the unknown,
                    of the future
that connected the past with the present,
to see what one cannot ordinarily see —

4.

The abstract crucifix
        to commemorate your father's passing,
the meeting of elbows
        in front of your ribcage,
the black bold sweep of cloth that sashays across
        like a flag detached
from a ship's broken mast —

all these find a centre,
a stillness
        that connect melting to melting,
soft as water, breath passing through
                every muscle in your body
as the dance freezes in the present's
                    final leap of faith,
and faith that carries the next act through.

5.

Soft as water
        you tread the ground
touching every tiny part of your feet's under-skin —

SEPARATION

Airport's large sliding glass doors separate us —
    you in the air-conditioned fake air-space inside
and I in the deluded dusty heat of Delhi outside.

There are transparent links that still bind us —
    the obviousness of wide-spanned glass-sheets;
my forgotten pair of prescription sun-glasses

left in your hide-skin hand-bag, dark green
    lenses sheltered in a dark green coffin-shaped
box, the one that you had to pass back to me

under the public glaring eyes of scrutiny;
    a wrapper-torn cylinder of shared Polo mints;
a child's parentage and the love for him.

These tercets contain lyrics of a dirge,
    imagined perhaps —
songs of happiness, stories of grief,

glue of memory, rumours of imagination,
    mishaps of short-circuit nerve-cells,
unskilled dangers of fantasy and ill-health.

My ultimate desire — a comforting aria, care,
    compassion, communion, friendship, and the
impractical constancy of my unconditional love.

8.
Blue Nude

An art which isn't based on feeling isn't art at all ...
Feeling is the principle, the beginning and end;
craft, objective, technique — all these are in the middle ....
— PAUL CÉZANNE

Every human being is a colony.
— PABLO PICASSO

Dreaming of Cezanne

THE CARDPLAYERS

The deal was done and stamped
   on the brown rough leather

of the parchment. The wooden
   table's crooked legs hardly held

its own weight,
   let alone the gravity of

smoke, spirit and connivance.
   We held our fists close

to each other as if in mistrust —
   stiff cards in hand

like little rectangular blades
   to cut and bleed our lives away.

The future like the present
   was dark and unlit, swirling

unsteadily in the tobacco stench
   permanently embedded

in the wood of the walls,
   the furniture, our clothes

and our hearts. But at least
   this was a gamble,

a zone of unsure light,
   an unpredictability

to hold onto amid all the grey,
   brown and blue,

cold, deep blue, and more blue.

[based on Cezanne's *Cardplayers*,
oil on canvas, 47.5 × 57 cm, 1893-96]

THE SKULLS

The three gods
   I worship
are dead.

   They stare
from the backs
   of their heads,

through
   the hollows
of their eyes —

   their vision
leaking from
   every fissure

and crack on
   the cranium.
The bone-skin

   of these skulls
shines like
   the breast sheen

of a new-born
   fish,
each plate

   like scales
restoring memory
   and genealogy —

secrets
   only fossils
keep alive.

   Skulls on wood,
on carpet,
   on drapery —

studies encrypted
    like
an unwrapped

    pyramid
of bones, mummies
    waiting

to be embalmed
    in oil and graphite —
as I sprinkle

water and colour
    on the shrine
of my night gods.

[based on Cezanne's series *The Skulls*,
oil on canvas / graphite and
watercolour on paper, 1890-1906]

JACKET ON A CHAIR

You carelessly tossed
    the jacket on a chair.
The assembly of cloth

    collapsed in slow motion
into a heap of cotton —
    cotton freshly picked

from the fields —
    like flesh
without a spine.

    The chair's wooden
frame provided a brief
    skeleton,

but it wasn't enough
    to renew the coat's
shape, the body's

    prior strength,
or the muscle
    to hold its own.

When one peels off
    one's outer skin,
it is difficult

    to hide
the true nature of
    blood.

Wood, wool, stitches,
    and joints —
an epitaph

    of a cardplayer's
shuffle,
    and the history

of my dark faith.

[based on Cezanne's *Jacket on a Chair*, graphite and watercolour on paper, 47.5 × 30.5 cm, 1890-92]

Picasso Triptych

HEAD I

My cranium
   stands
fossilised
   and
triangulated
   on the
black 'T'
   of a
crucifix.
   The blue
and white
   crescent
and head's
   hemisphere,
sit askance
   in their
bone-sharp
   intentions.
It was Breton
   who had
scripted
   the line-
breaks, and
   the cell's
own narrative.

[based on Pablo Picasso's *Head* (1913).
Paper collage, charcoal & pencil on card.]

HEAD II

My imagination
   is cupped
entirely in
   the creased palms
of my hands —
   lepered,
folded, and bronzed —
   encased
and colonised
   within
anaesthetic clarity
   of a
transparent cube.
   But don't you see,
it is trying to
   reach out —
to feel you —
   even though
it is only
   an imagination
of love
   contained in
the heart's
   own sleeve.

[based on Pablo Picasso's *The Head or Arm with Sleeve* (1948). Bronze.]

HEAD III

   Plasmaic,
the green amoeba
   resembles
my hair,
   that has
collected silt
   and humour
for centuries.
   My eyes, lips,
cheeks, nostrils —
   all pink
in the white
   semen of life.
Only blue
   provides me
with hope,
   and blue,
and death —
   and blue.

[based on Pablo Picasso's
Head (1971). Pastel on paper.]

Matisse Sequence

WOMAN WITH AMPHORA

Unpasting herself
   from the deep
blue of the sky,
   she rises
and walks gently
   towards me,
bearing
   on her head
an earthen jar
   containing
the mysteries
   of fresh amphora.
Her shadow
   stretches
disappearing
   into the blue,
then reappears,
   long and elegant
dreaming
   of Giacometti.
Just as she comes
   into focus,
she freezes
   within
her tall frame
   holding the thaw
of her contents,
   the perfume
escaping
   just enough
to make me
   want more.

[based on Henri Matisse's
Femme a l'amphora, 1953]

WOMAN WITH AMPHORA
AND POMEGRANATES

Having stolen
  the blue
from the sky's
  canvas
for her own body,
  she stands
in statuesque
  elegance,
arms stretched
  in two half-arcs,
guarding
  the secret
of her amphora.
  The guarded jar
allows
  four pomegranates
to spill
  and tumble
in pairs,
  fertilising
the family
  that remain.
The image
  incomplete
in its
  completeness.

[based on Henri Matisse's
Femme a l'amphora et grenades, 1953]

CREATION

The myth of creation
   makes us believe —
woman was created
   from man's rib.
Or was it
   monkey's rib
that man
   was created from?
Or, was monkey
   created
from fruit, from
   pomegranate-rain?
Resting, stretching,
   dancing, tumbling,
women and monkeys
   germinate —
creation of (wo)man
   kind.

[based on Henri Matisse's *Femmes et singes*, 1952]

STANDING BLUE NUDE

Below colourless clouds,
   she lies on white sand,
her hands bent backwards,
   her two palms
overlapping
   to support the back
of her nape and head.

Or is she standing up,
   stretching after
passion has ebbed?
   Invisible expressions
of her face and body,
   still-blue, silent
with the cool of love.

[based on Henri Matisse's *Nu bleu debout*, 1952]

SATI

She waits
   at the feet
of her
   husband's
pyre,
   stacking
the last
   pieces:
wood, memory,
   and tears.
The slow
   fire
lights up
   her glassy
eyes,
   her stripped
body,
   and soul.
The smoke
   in loops
of arc,
   frames
the ritual,
   a ceremony
that leaves
   only
the dead alive,
   and
the live, dead.

[inspired by Henri Matisse's
Baigneuse dans les roseaux, 1952]

SINE CURVE

    The sine-curve's
undulating curvature

    defies
the equation's

    evenness.
Here, white,

    off-white, and blue
play out

    a sequence,
unevenly symmetrical,

    leading gently to
a feminine

    ending.
Only in this instance,

    what's vague
retains clarity

    and definition,
the four

    split into three
segments — half,

    three, and half.
It's the leading

    half
and the trailing

    half
that dictates

    rhythm,
it's improvisation

    that makes
the vague

    very definite
and womanly.

[based on Henri Matisse's *La Vague*, 1952]

BLUE NUDE
SKIPPING ROPE

   She skips
her way
  to
womanhood,
   twisting
the rope
   into plaits,
body
   into sex,
white
   into blue,
gentleness
   into motion.
She springs
   into play —
her small
   breasts,
her thin
   waist,
her heavy
   thighs —
oozing
   the weight
of sweat
   and milk.

[based on Henri Matisse's
Nu bleu, sauteuse de corde, 1952]

BLUE NUDE I

Resting nude, crouched and leaning light
   against a transparent wall, her right

thigh and calf clamps her left ankle tight, as
   her left hand mirrors the same clasp

gently over the other. The right limb, outstretched,
   free, over her head, welcomes the fresh

warm penetrating sun, as she allows it to stroke her
   body lavishly after the long winter,

eliminating any shadow that might have gathered within
   her folds. She sits statue-still, pondering in

the azure haze of reflected light from a pool of water,
   beside the blue of her heart, the Krishna

of her thoughts frozen ice-blue on the pale canvas —
   a languid broken figure, a cut-and-paste focus.

[based on Henri Matisse's
Nu bleu I, 1952]

BLUE NUDE II

    Gently she has shifted her alloted space
this time, and with it
    the supine arch of her grace,
the soft-posture tempering her inter-locking

    limbs and body, the sun, and the art
itself. But this sun's apogee
    has disappeared, unlighting the parts
previously lit by passion's heat.

    It's burnt ends, now slowly gathering
pace. Up-close, she looks flushed when kissed,
    but from afar, her changing
mood is too subtle and hardly noticed.

    The cut-and-paste may alter its clarity,
but never her skin's bare purity.

[based on Henri Matisse's
Nu bleu II, 1952]

BLUE NUDE III

    Perfectly posed, poised
as if for a fashion shoot,
    she appears well-trained

in this art, as her sisters
    in the other three frames
by contrast, remain amateurs.

    Her back perfectly arched,
her upper and lower torso
    positioned to receive

adulation and lust, a desire
    that's painted only
on the onlooker's face,

    subtly hidden in their
brows, lashes, and gaze.

[based on Henri Matisse's
Nu bleu III, 1952]

BLUE NUDE IV

    Her nursed figure is mere memory,
a memory of war, of recollection
    through a museum of images,
a photograph: blue on sepia, cut,
    pasted, engraved, its edges frayed
and dissolved — her elbow chewed out
    by explosives, her toe bearing

only three digits — statistics
    of war, ruthless. Her arched body,
now remains frozen as sculpture,
    a memorial to passion, patience,
and pain. In peace-time, her torn
    memories wage war, even though
the flawless sun, shines on her blues.

[based on Henri Matisse's
Nu bleu IV, 1952]

Four Watercolours

RAILWAY STATION, BOMBAY

The coolie's red jacket
   partially hides
his blackened bones,

ones that show their fate
   under white wrappings
of *dhoti* and turban.

He leap-frogs at you
   with an electric sense
of urgency,

as you stumble out
   with your own baggage.
Preconceptions rage

rampant here,
   thick and heavy
in the stale humid air.

Slavery and commerce
   jostle for their own
space. There is no room

for small kindnesses.
   Only images captured
by sable-hair's

trained ends, stroked
   on hand-made paper
and glazed lacquer,

can afford to drown
   their sorrows
in water and dye.

LODI GARDENS, DELHI

In this medieval
    burial ground, a dynasty
preserves its fading

grace. The grass, smooth
    as a *pashmina* shawl,
carpets the brittle soil.

Here, under the watchful
    eye of the mausoleum —
now lonely with disuse —

young lovers make out
    their own space and
sense of new history,

lie in each others arms,
    calm and agitated,
in the dead still of heat.

UDAIPUR, RAJASTHAN

On the desert sands,
    a man and his wife
balanced tentatively

on a riot-torn bicycle,
    chance a ride —
its precariousness

safer than the routine
    gamble of their own
lives. The only solace

resides in the invisible
    folds of the night-wind,
one that erases the daily

tread, hiding their story.
    In the distance, across
tinted glass-mirage,

Udaipur Lake reflects
    its quiet fate,
as dusk pastel-coats

the fort's Rajput façade,
    to make some sense
of its own past.

ELM PARK LANE, LONDON

Amid the studio's
   book-stacked warmth,
finished images

cry out to escape
   the posh transparence
of silicate-safe

confines, their own
   colour-washed truths
defying the framed

uneven matt
   of varnished wood.
Watercolours

by nature, are born
   to bleed —
to accommodate secrets

incomplete pictures
   leave untold —
to allow for our own

unstated desires,
   and the blood's
inadequate crimsom.

DALI'S PÂTE DE VERRE

Glass-pink sweep of the neck's nape —
it's missing shape like an absent mannequin
        mimics complications of an empty hanger —
the hollow hold of a death-mask.

As gravity pulls down metal silicates
        to gather in a clayey-bronze lump —
orange changes to green
                to brown to black —
        its shine and shape
hiding their crystal impulse.

Is it a hat on a disturbed face
                whose silhouette stores
        angst of the subconscious —
transcending dreams that only artists can dream,
        dreams no psychoanalysis is able to solve.

Light in this sculpture's hollow tunnel
    collects
        as if in a telescope's virtual cylinder —
it doesn't magnify the image
    but calibrates
the volume of light in cold storage —
        so we can see better, the same image.

The Persistence of Memory
        changes from canvas to glass paste —
        pâte de verre melts, boils, and cools —
the crystal-finish wearing an elegant
                nonchalance of *Venus de Milo* —
marble-touch feigning glass.

Baudelaire's *Fleur du Mal* scan
        introvertedly
marking Dali's homage to Daum —
                poetry put through the prose
of glass-making emerges anew, wax-like.

Obsession, dream, desire —
>   hyper-rational blending irrational with
>   a bi-polar lyric in multiple tongues —
hollow, transparent, opaque, solid —
>   and always crystal sharp.

[based, in part, on Dali's *Le désir hyperrationnel*, 1984,
Pâte de verre and bronze | Collection of the Salvador Dalí Museum]

DRAWING KAFKA OUT

I lean against this hollow picture frame
that sketches and mirrors my transparent image.
  Holding onto one of its pedestal supports,

I realise this crucifix has a reflected 'real-one'
  on the other side, balancing the entire prop.
The only thing here not in reflected-doubles

  are my legs, but they don't need mirrors
or things in pairs at a time — they are born twins
  to be solitary and familial, simultaneously.

Kafka stares at me gauging my intent. These are
  strange times — words fit
only for *an emergency kit*. I cry out loud,

  "Franz, there is enough bloody illusion
to destroy everyone's psyche". He pauses a while
  and declares, "Then re-set this *mis en scene*."

[based on an illustration by Franz Kafka]

CHAGALL CHANCEL

Jesus towers over Mary
    in tropical-green incandescence —
framed by panels — ink-blue and gold.
    The Prophets, Jacob, Christ,
Zion, Law — all stand upright,

their pride lapping our adoration
    and their own narcissism —
misplaced, burdened
    under the correctness
of politics, colour, and geography.

While the lesser gods bide time
    waiting in the wings —
tinted citrus-red and turquoise —
    their moment of flight
dictated by the presiding god,

and the soul of the crucifix.
    Thousand jig-saws, pieced together,
woven in uneven segments —
    a loose-leafed narrative,
hide-bound — modern, sparse,

biblical, gilt-edged —
    a psychedelic
confusion of order and sanctity.
    Lambs keep peace,
as do the angels.

Rainbow of red, orange, amber,
    and ochre,
their secret inherent dye —
    blood-mark and baptise
dynasty, hierarchy, and station.

Heat is coolly preserved
    in thermometric lengths —
a quintet of translucent flutes —
    stained mosaic, ink, iridium,
tempered glass, and subdued light.

Only the solemn modernity
    of this chapel-space
and our human-breath
    keeps the reality
of fantasy and illusion intact,

kept even more still
    in this wavering sea-air,
by controlled transparence
    of moving faith, and
subtlety of altering architecture.

*[inspired by Marc Chagall's 'Chancel Stained
Windows' (1970), Fraumunster, Zurich].*

❦

AMISTAD

1.
The dead white
drags the black alive,

along the ridge
of the slanted coffin,

his one hand
pointing to the sky,

the other
chained to hell.

2.
A requiem
chopped out

of the waves —
a tall elongated

crucifix of a frame,
a clear frieze,

struck,
by white lightning.

[based on a painting by Tom Feeling]

ROTÉ FABRIK PAINTINGS

The framed sandscapes
   under the arc-lights inside,

glow red, orange, and gold,
   deceiving

the cold silver waves
   on Lake Zurich outside,

and the watery moon
   afloat in the night's

translucent sky.
   Shapes on the canvas

without names,
   objects without

an object,
   textures sculpted

in subtle undulations
   reveal landscapes

of many lands, emotions
   of many hearts,

many coded colours
   that spark and change,

depending on the power
   of the electric watt,

or imagined sunlight.
   With altering light,

the colours change,
   so does the text,

inner soul inert
   though alive to touch,

waiting for the point
   where the prepared bristles

spread out and expand
   in strands,

radiant in wet spaces —
   moisture, oil, silicates —

all merge defying their densities.
   Submerged shapes

of ephemeral squares and triangles
   defy the plasmaic spread

of acrylic space, a cosmos
   converging, diverging

in a slow-spreading
   blot of creation.

The studio's bright
   stark wall inside

and the dark lake outside,
   stand separated

in unison,
   by a historic wall —

graffiti-stained, red-bricked —
   that values time and art,

expatriated
   in heat-retaining silicates

that eventually radiate,
   later

emerging from exile
   in time-lapse exposures.

*[inspired, in part, by the sandscape
paintings of Prafull Davé]*

COVER DRAWING

1.

A medieval master-key,
    now rusted;

clay jars,
    weathered black;

disused pots;
    uneven rafters;

picture frames —
    all hide behind

weaves and weaves
    of cobweb hair,

their silver gossamer
    wrapping

everything
    in wide gentle

sweeps of parabola,
    arcs that contain

a preserved narrative.

2.

A young goddess,
    armed with many hands,

sits askance within
    the crooked wooden

termite-carved frame,
    surprised at her own

turquoise halo.
    Even this mere splash

of beatific blue
    amid black, white

and grey, appears
    kaleidoscopic.

Against light,
    this world-view

refracts
    another story — and

yet another, at night.

3.

There lives life
    among the dead here,

and death lurks
    in untrampled spaces

coming alive
    at the subtle stroke

of human hands.
    But this woman's

kohl-edged pupils stare,
    transforming the blue

into a blazing gaze,
    scorching the silver

web-strings to change
    their arc, the curves

arching their spine
    to form

yet another drawing.

4.

Here, only metaphors
    matter,

as do tenuous lines —
  their religion

and passion.
    I try to contain

my secrets
    and their luxuries

quietly within
    the jagged edges

of sheet-pulp,
    but the vivid blue

and the glistening
    silk-strands

spiral out,
    exploding secretly,

in uncontrolled helixes.

*[inspired by a painting
by Imtiaz Dharker]*

COW-DUST HOUR

The storm clouds are heavy and livid
sucking all the fire from the earth's belly.

The blues are fast disappearing
giving way to monsoon's inherent strength.

When the skies bow to fire,
it must mean anger or hate —

but in this soft hour when cows
return home from the pastures

hoofing up fine red-dust in the air
marking an auspicious *godhuli lagna* —

it must mean passion or yearning instead;
a force so strong that it quietly stretches

and redefines the definition of canvas,
geometry, landscape, and the seasons.

[inspired by a Rokeya Sultana painting]

ENGLISH COLOURS

Banana green's
  fluorescent tinge
competes with yellow

and glazed bright
  olive
in your kitchen.

Bottles — various
  shapes and sizes
placed tentatively —

transparent
  and in varying
shades of green.

Upstairs, cream
  complements blue.
Cream walls, carpets,

blinds, pine, cloth,
  and more bottles —
transient blues,

squares, cylinders.
  Candles secretly left
in unexpected corners,

in jars — unburnt, virgin,
  to be burnt later
perhaps, at the stakes.

Suburbia's quiet pastels,
  its silent music
makes me restless.

I go out for a walk,
  there is more beauty
in the grey cold rains.

Inside on the shelves
  there is order,
perfect alphabetical order —

the Anvils, Bloodaxes,
    Fabers — all grouped
for safety's sake,

lest a foreign metaphor
    alters the balance
of this English island.

But my unspent
    passion spills colour
coating my fantasies,

permanently casting
    my translucent paint
on crisp laser sheets.

At least this helps
    temporarily to prop up
my body heat,

lest it drops
    perilously low, when
danger and reliance

on chemical colours
    are the only ways
to inject crimson

back into my life.
    But I don't have
any such fears here,

there are enough
    hues to create
a whole monolith —

to cover in its entirety
    Ayers rock
with folk art.

It is the intensity
    and chaos
I crave for and miss.

SHADOWS OF BLACK

I slice open my expectant womb — instead of red, I find the deep dark space of space. The comma of an embryo is gone, the vein's grammar frayed, the corpuscles anaemic —

all mapping the ultrasound of a cosmos — black, delicate black, black with subtle patterns, square folds of black in neat sequences where the measure of texture is the gradation of shadow, shadows the black casts onto itself.

There is relief, topographical relief — *shikishi* contours with invisible white streaks, flurries, semen wisps, hair-like trails of a shooting star that appear to bless the blind to see black, black in its utmost clarity —

deep-sea sonar sounds, breath sounds trapped in amniotic fluid — all assemble themselves as the most exquisite chamber music, cast within the shadows of black.

❧

MOTH, ART

Night slices through my morning's horizon with tentativeness — it is struggling to capture and gather dawn's elusive light.

A white moth traces hyperbolic arcs against this unsure canvas where light shifts each and every second. The canvas is made not of linen, but of sky's transparence — appearing as if through a vast panoramic lens. I am unsure of its focal-length. It mimics the new technology "varifocals" mapping retina's power, its indices changing with the minutest mathematical distance.

All these and the change in cloud-density, make the moth's intricate line-work a fluid form, an artwork too difficult to trace — beautifully controlled white lines on dark canvas.

Along comes another moth, a female one chased by a kite. It is wooing of the most perverse kind. Without any notice or care, the kite swoops into her body splattering red ink. White death covered with red life — a miniaturist's delight that takes flight only when one is most unprepared.

Triptych[3]

FEAST
hope is a thing with feathers
— EMILY DICKINSON

1. BIRTH

That final focused
   piercing ray,

that sudden flash
   of pin-pointed light

that sparks love —
   sex embalming,

cracking open —
   feasting a new birth.

2. AFTER-LIFE

On the mirror-shelf,
   a broken egg-shell

left asunder
   with a hint

of congealed blood,
   dead in its cusp.

An errant feather
   trying its best to fly

resists its instinct
   to take off —

instead, chooses
   to remain

static in this
   windless space.

All this under
   the gaze

of high wattage
   severity —

birth-light
   imprinting its genes.

3. MIRROR

Memory reflects
   the past

into the present's
   future.

Mirror, feather, shell —
   glass, lens, light —

shadows define what is
   otherwise hidden,

unspoken, unlit
   in this bright light.

[Poems on pages 170 & 171 are based on the art of Manisha Gera Baswani]

ACRYLIC

1.

My hands are still dripping — with paint, with swirling fumes and cry of acrylic, with colours emanating smell of seductive chemical. It was the first time I had faced a real canvas mounted on its easel and been presented with an array of acrylics to choose from at will. And before I could get to grips with this medium — the physicality of brushes, sable hair, scalpel, palette, ceramic bowls, tubes of paint, and a blank canvas — something induced me to jump head-long into the act, without practice, with my heart doing the talking; ... just like a child who stares wide-eyed and thrilled at opening a box of new toys; ... just like a blind person whose sight has been recently restored from the unfocussed monochromatic to a vision that is kaleidoscopic.

I had come here to explore a new medium in art as catharsis. I had chosen, in my mind, the colours I wanted to use — deep blue and white — before I had even arrived here. All I wanted was a stretch of virgin linen where I could layer my coded narratives; try at the same time, to express and hide.

2.

As I walked into my friend's gleaming white apartment, I was warmed by the unannounced ambience that they had created — with the profusion of natural greens, ferns and leaves; ... with the quietly kept pair of glass bowls — one containing molten shapes of coloured wax, and the other, an assembly of match-boxes from all over the world; ... with well framed paintings hung judiciously on the walls; ... with books and CDs that lay in perfect geometric arrangement on carpets and shelves — all suitably lit and positioned.

There I was, facing a well-appointed canvas — pristine in its white undercoat — a near-perfect *tabula rasa*. I had come here to paint the monsoons in blues and whites.... I had come here to hide the subtle rift between the two Bengals under layers of paint.... I had come here to assuage my deep-seated grief of the loss of a child.

But by the time I left the studio, I had before me — colours running riot on a grainy canvas space, texture and undulation creating relief against the frozen density of paint, narratives torn asunder from Bengali newsprint, red and white strings providing anchor and balance, an errant feather arrested in mid-flight, white tissues trying their best to absorb blood, and more — all these on a vertical piece of stretched linen, an untutored map, a previously uninhabited terrain.

3.

Late that evening, at the day's end, as I sat sweating and exhausted in the frenzy of paint, pondering upon the canvas I had just created, staring at the shapes and stories it contained — I could hear, with gathering intensity, the prayer call outside — *Allah-u-Akbar, Allah-u-Akbar.*

ANISH KAPOOR
diptych

1. MY SIGHT

Curvatures
              have a seductive way
of making slow-motion love.

Smooth of the nape —
              the mirrored parabolas —
incarnadine corpuscle-spurts on white —
      relentless, poised.

Refractive index
            pushed to its limit.

A narrative of possibilities
      held
            in metal-glass globes
inverting mirror-lines
to deceive horizon's balance.

Imagine blue —
deepest blues folding inward —
              in womb-like convolutions

where life's emergence and extinction
            are a science and an art,
      engineering subtle miniature
compositions.

Longitude and latitudes
              stretched out
            as a vertical steel sheet —
an elastic band
      only to be released —
               tsunami sine-waves
on 'z' axis.

Primal colours glow
      in their incandescence

eventually
>>>>captured in metal —
glazed to the best sheen —

a reflection of
>>>>you|me, inside|outside,
>>>>upside down,
each flicker
>>>>an acute-angle inflection of
a heartbeat.

❦

2. HIS WORK

The void, the crack, the flesh
>>>>has no place in the oval pavilion —
landscape [a] void —

Cloud gate — kissing bridge —
>>>>draws us in to the navel
imagining Naples Subway leading
to similar spaces.

An oval transposed
>>>>in-out.

Temenos —
>>>>fishing nets pulled cylindrical
>>>>>>as horizontal mesh —
gauze-like transparency
>>>>mapped on Spire and chasm —
>>>>sea mirror, mirror heaven, water-vortex —

heavenly syntax. Melancholia's second coming
>>>>building for a void.

When I am pregnant —
>>>>my body healing
the black earth, >>mother as a mountain
>>>>>>as a thousand names bloom.

YUKI

In Japanese, Yuki is snow —
    unmelted and poised.

She sits askance
    in front of a wine-tinged door

whose paint flakes
    to expose its wood-raw skin —

pale, seemingly snow-flecked.
    Her hair rambles all over

her face, eyes, and neck,
    as she stares shyly —

sideways into the distance.
    There are secrets locked,

bolted securely
    in a shut non-descript studio

in Mumbai,
    tucked away somewhere

in Prabha Devi —
    as the industrial estate

temporarily quietens
    at the allusive

thought of snow herself.
    Fantasy instils in

factory-workers, passion —
    just as for me —

peeling curls of paint,
    a circular chromium lock,

a rusted dis-used bolt,
    and breeze that affects

a woman's hair and lashes,
    inspires visions

of snow —
    thaw, compassion, desire.

[based on a photo by Rafeeq Ellias]

🐾

SAINT SEBASTIAN

No, I'm not Saint Sebastian.
    I am the naked metaphorical
white man strapped and pierced
    by arrows of condescension,
bleeding not out of agony,
    but out of irreverence for
and ignorance of the 'other'.

[based on the painting 'Saint Sebastian'
by Gerrit van Honthorst, 1590 —1656]

RED RAIN

Chopped wood —
    stacked, floating, dead.

An idle boat —
    rudderless, adrift.

Black rain,
    red rain —

but not a drop
    to drink or taste.

No space left
    for humans —

only beauty
    of contamination —

like rainbows
    and sunsets —

prolongs illusion.
    It is illusion

that allows us
    to live, dream —

charting out our own
    perpetual diary.

[based on a photo by Tanvir Fattah]

THE VORTEX |
THE JOURNEY TO THE CENTRE OF THE EARTH

*From a circle to a point, bindu .... it disappears to shunya,
nothing. From this nothingness life begins again
and becomes everything, the total universe.*   — P.M.

I started my painting, journeying on the edges of periphery,
    unnoticed and unthreatened, mapping my way with words
to the centre, on this linen-stitched terrain, untrained,

where the colour gold made love to the blackness of coal,
    where blue and yellow merged but couldn't emerge as green,
where red's innate passion could not subdue the demure blue;

where the madness of the border and the sanity of the centre
    were at constant war, not knowing whether
the insanity belonged to the centre or sanity to the border.

I plotted and plodded along, stroking soft sable hair
    against the circular ridges of a Martian moon, the Chandrama
helping to examine its own grains and its quartzite glaze.

Here I realised, to understand death, one has to understand life,
    to know darkness, one needs to know light itself,
to see colour, one has to see through white, and what it contains.

Our vision is a fragment in the vast space of undisclosed colours,
    our sight, limited to what we see, limitless to what we imagine,
but our mind's eye is still under the presiding Goddess's *bindu*.

I like my life on the margins of history having tasted the love-lipped
    vortex of the centre: its transient power of seduction and revulsion,
its elasticity that pulls and expels with the same equative power.

I like the periphery: it has more space at its edges,
    more room to breathe and create, more room to perish unnoticed,
more room to colour and grow as one pleases and more honesty, like

its circular ripples that expand and ebb, remaking uncharted waves.
    After all, without the orbit, how can the centre exist,
without the circumference, how can the circle itself, live?

[based on a painting by Prafulla Mohanty]

IRIS

Pebbles placed on paper on a secluded beach —
white sheets torn from your and my diaries
of the past
        to record the present, the future.

        The story followed —
magnetically mapping a trail of disengaged sheets
        linked by stones — various shapes
weighing them down — and their narrative —

🌱

As I danced to one of my favourite old French tunes,
I heard the waters of the sea
        lapping in the background —

I thought of words, their connections,
their logic and meaning, their meaninglessness —
        and the companionship they privately provide.

🌱

As age set in, so did your Indian ways —
the subtle *pranaam* — hands clasped in welcome
        and joy —

🌱

In spite of Englishness, and 'so-called' infidelities —
        both feminine and masculine ...
and the wondrous penumbra that lies therein —
        John's love for you remained steadfast
even though "[we]re lost ... and [you] d[id]n't care" —
but I did, and I knew deep down that you did too —

        "You *are* my world ..."
and I loved you "little mouse,
        [and] I know you do too", said JB.
And you ... *oh* ....
        Was I dreaming ... in present tense?

🌱

Even after reams of texts, novels,
            and so much more,
you grappled with the basics of memory
                and thought, and instinct —

She was so … *so* very quiet when she died,
I wouldn't have minded
                a little bit of that — myself.

[inspired, in part, by Richard Eyre's film 'Iris']

❦

AUGUST RHAPSODY

I can hear electricity travel
                as chime-sounds do
in light breeze.

There are millions of chimes
                like millions of stars
lighting millions of miles
                for sight.

An electric spark
                      fires my pupils
              to blindness,
blindness
that sees through all —
              shut eye's wide vision.

It is the month of August,
            the month I was born —
    electric-rush,   womb-scores,
            neurons sparking notes,
lyrics song.

Silent tunes are loud,   melody quiet
and crackle-charged —
as sheet music melts   hot current.

[inspired by the film, 'August Rush']

FREEHOLD | LEASEHOLD

At an impossible right-angle
                      on a totem pole top,
your scrawny bronze elbow
        supports your gait and flight
of imagination —
            visions of Maiya — a woman arched,
frozen in a reverse summersault.

She is writing
        the beginnings of an epic
on top of another column —
        a column bearing a gaggle
                  of people-miniatures —
crowded like a field
        of tall reeds in sway, Giacometti-like —
all pasted along its length.

And yet she is alone, as he is,
                staring askance,
each perched on two opposing poles —
        polarities that rarely match or meet these days,
the same polarities that were once an attraction.

You now say that
            romantic love disappears
    in a long marriage,
yet I do not understand
            such a grave pronouncement
borne with such nonchalance.
It saddens me deeply to hear of it.

Unlike yours,
        for me love only thickens over time,
romance strengthens,
                intimacy intensifies.

Love is not on leasehold
                that it expires like a contract —
            but after hearing you, I feel that it might be.

Yet I am like Maiya
        writing her poem against all odds,
            against gravity,
and you like Musui
        only a gazer of the arts,
            able to detach and attach
to suit your self — consume when needed,
and discard when not.

Those born with a freehold contract
        cannot change to leasehold deeds.
            I only wish the details of deeds
were spelled out when we first met.

Poets like artists are prone
        to the minutest change in weather —
how else would Maiya and Musui
            leap with such extravagance?

Vast installation in bronze,
            metal flying in perpetual motion —
        there is clamour, there is passion,
there is touch,
people's hands up and outstretched
        skywards, celebrating
            mood, desire, and yearning.

Love's freehold does not come free,
or without pain.
Maiya and Musui look at each other,
then away —
a tear drops, and she begins to bleed.

[based, in part, on K S Radhakrishnan's
Freehold Musui, bronze, 96cms × 211cms, 2005]

ENTROPY

Curved nape of china-white porcelain
   sweeps circumstance formed by touch.

Your fingers have many stories to tell
   as you shape ceramic one by one —

sometimes similar, other times dissimilar —
   subtle variance of tone and texture.

You like being with family, among friends,
   so your pieces are never alone;

though they find homes in lonely places —
   given your arrangement's unique

displacements, allocations —
   on derelict factory floors and piers;

on mossy flights of disused steps
   that might lead into a stagnant canal

as corroded handrails keep balance;
   on sea-cliff faces where bowls are birds

waiting for the waves to crash in —
   vessels toppling into foam, featherless.

You allow porcelain to be rearranged,
   stolen, broken —

as long as passion remains the same
   as the original flush of sex

when it was first conceived
   and made, your dreams first glazed.

A lone black bowl
   amid an array of white disappears

one night, only to reappear dutifully
   in a straight line

perched on the rugged rust-peels
   of an abandoned pipeline.

Others lie under the unequal rain
   of shattered glass,

thick shards from large windows
   that creak to open, but do not close.

Some line up like empty spice jars
   on metal rivets hanging

on poured concrete, waiting —
   buildings never to be built.

Yet others trail off to a stony outcrop
   or to the sea sand-wash,

or stay tarmac-spread
   in square grids on country roads

no one seems to cross,
   where a shut wooden gate stands vigil.

Or they lie
   buried in snow, white on white.

Very few are privileged
   with the care of comfort's warmth —

sterling silver wrapping spoon-like,
   cold clinging for contact.

But there is always gentle movement
   in your craft's apparent stasis.

As the maker lets her off-springs fly
   she relinquishes control, allowing

these whites to create their own colour,
   own shape, own narratives

in their broken altered states.
   It is an art of abandonment,

of cartography, of geometry —
   a slow-shifting canvas for entropy.

[inspired by Megan Randall installations]

YOUR FLIGHT

is like a goddess with transparent wings
    transforming paper into swathes —
tall grass swaying in angular breeze.

Monochrome reeds keep within their folds
    many secrets of creation.
But that splash, that hint of red, that bird

transforms everything — still-frame to life,
    life to laughter, laughter to lines stringing
a soundless song of sanity.

And all along you wait for your sorrow to heal,
    sorrow that death of a loved one brings.
Snow on the ground remains persistent

delaying closure. So we pray
    to the snow that is stubbornly unforgiving,
snow that is too hard to cut.

Suddenly, the etched bird frozen red
    on your litho-space decides to fly —
paper's rough-edged terrain tear

at their edges. A new song seduces her away —
    a flight beyond limits, a ritual burial
defying gravity's slow pull. It took just a bird

claw to etch ice, to engrave its glass-wings
    with italicised initials of your own,
to resuscitate, to inject new life.

A lyric born of broken wings
    knitted feather by feather, bone by bone,
scale matched by tenor of 'love walks'

in an open country that feels like home.
    Bird song — reed-stalk, beak-nib,
grass-palette, and snow's polar light.

9.
GEOGRAPHIES

In the great square
*The prolonged vowel of silence
Makes itself heard.*
— DOM MORAES, 'Absences'

*I am like sand in the hourglass
which can be time only in falling.*
— ANA BLANDIANA

HAWTHORNDEN SUITE (*extracts*)

CAVES

… she deserts the night
Hid in a vacant, interlunar cave.
— JOHN MILTON, *Samson Agonistes [I]*

The double-bolted lock on the iron-studded door kept the secret of the caves intact. Upon entering, I realized I had come here before, before I was born. I remembered everything vividly — the long low-ceilinged corridor with a room on the left, and another at the end on the right.

Also at the end was the cave's mouth that opened its jaws onto the glen and the swirling Esk below. Standing there, my eyes were led by a strong shaft of sunlight that illuminated another passageway on the left.

That in turn led to another view of the outside, and adjacent to it, a pockmarked room. Here old, short bottles of brew were once stored in uneven squarish niches etched into the wall — each like a pigeonhole for ancient scrolls to be preserved as clues for later inhabitants.

Honeycombs expanded their space, their vision — circular sockets turning into squares, reducing the third dimension to a flat-walled grid. It was a new matrix, one that included depth and gravity, unpretension and humanity.

Light played out a whole play in the space of a short act — each square in the matrix on the wall echoing unlinked verses, passages that needed to be read and traversed until dream and reality merged into one.

Each niche had a different wavelength, a different tone, a different texture. The damp indicated a recent dweller's attempt to etch hieroglyphs, but she had run out of ink.

That is when she discovered the hidden well, one that appeared halfway down to hell. I had peered down its neck from the castle garden yesterday, and now I stood midway on its tunnel-descent — static waters stored ink for an invisible parchment that lived in these innocuous squares.

The ink-water had to be siphoned from the earth under the granite, from the belly of Esk's riverbed through the well's cylinder — stored until it fermented — with moss, bird droppings, spider weavings, deadwood, chipped granite tempered with human blood and bat juice — and produced invisible text of astonishing clarity.

The narrative shone in the golden evening light, but when I lit my torchlight against it, each and every letter of the italicized script magically evaporated, leaving the walls without any imprint.

I had discovered the art of calligraphy down here — the elegance of the slanted hand, the trills of wide loops, and the subtlety of serifs — its ascenders, descenders and ligatures. I'd also learned to value graphite and its secret erasures, and ink with its indelible invisibility.

If you could breathe the air down here, you could decode the text and paint its arches; otherwise your fate was sealed in the dungeon under the weight of formal words.

Outside, there were crimson petals strewn on the fresh green of the undergrowth. It was as if one of the cave's inhabitants had left her secrets in them — menstrual bleed, now clotted as dry petals, rich in mineral — containing the narrative of her entire life.

༈

CASTLE WALK

A pillared shade
High overarched, and echoing walks between
— JOHN MILTON, *Paradise Lost [IX, 1106]*

The Castle Walk began gently, taking me away from the heavy stones into the woods. Trees, plants and shrubbery with their dense verdant over-arches filtered the sky's light into a pale consistent green.

It was cool and calm there — the only sounds were those of birds, the river, and my feet's shuffle and squelch on the path.

The path's gravel changed to dirt, dirt to mud, mud to a carpet of lichen. The carpet's subtle weave and colour changed — fern-like, rounded, serrated — grey, brown, green.

And before long the path swept around, taking you close to Esk's banks, running along side by side, but keeping a distance of mutual safety.

As I approached the base of the castle, two severe rock faces checked my approach. Their skin was bold, weathered, defined by deep elegant striations. Wind, water, cold and heat had carved their individual signatures on them. Every niche and inch of the rocks had a changing character — mineral red, moss green, granite brown — smooth, rough, jagged. They even assumed the shape and profile of the characters I imagined, changing their contours with the change of my heart. Both death and fecundity loomed large there — nitrogen fuelling their quiet activity.

I stumbled upon a patch of cream-coloured mushrooms — their abundant spores attracting pheromones in vast numbers. They had both a coy and confident look about them, a stance that could be as deceptive as their intent and the velvet touch of their virile predatory skin.

Finally, I came to the end — to the red tree where the fox was sighted the other day. The tree's wide-skirted crown of leaves looked like a feathery parasol, lip-red lace intricately tracing patterned imprint of oak on each leaf.

I collected some of them that lay on the soil, shed by the force of the afternoon's rain. They were glistening as the pupils of people do, when they have just died. There was something definite and defiant about their composure — a lifetime mapped in each and every vein — no regrets, no ill-will, just the magic of capillary action that transmits the glint of its bright crimson to the farthest and most searching eyes.

Red, the colour appeared once again. Ultimately, rouge delicacy underlined all that was valuable. There was grace and humility in impermanence.

DUNGEON

> *... upon the vapour of a dungeon, ...*
> — WILLIAM SHAKESPEARE, *Othello [III.iii.271]*

Today I visited the dungeon again to look for Cézanne's bones. The rusty weight of the iron hatch resisted my efforts to lift up the darkness. But a spider weaving a new web nearby assisted me with her invisible pull of silver strings.

An oxidized ladder peeling crimson-brown metal dropped in, straight like a plumb line, the 'y' axis graded equally against the 'x' on its descent.

I lowered myself — more spiders assisted, welcoming me with garlands of gauze-wet gossamer. This somewhat distracted me from the dank deeds of the dead.

I focused my thoughts on aspects of architecture — the seemingly disappearing arches holding the belly of the castle, the disappearing perspective of a lone window wanting desperately to woo the sky, the strained linings of my lungs in this receding faint air.

Everything had a purpose and a plan — each grid, each matrix, each web — providing space in three dimensions. Depth, distance and height were hard to judge. I had to measure time only by sound — by its tonality and register.

The clatter of bones sounded their hollow as I carelessly shuffled my feet in the darkness. I could feel I had crushed a femur accidentally, as its texture changed from brittle to powder against the rough granite of the floor.

I had come looking for a holograph of Cézanne's will and skulls, but what I found instead was a score — an opera with the aria highlighted.

The entire orchestration was vivid — stringed instruments, gossamer strings — and flute — wind fluting down a remote window, gathering bone dust into whispers.

CROSSING TONGUES

Jade of the deepest seas —
   your names spell out
the meaning of pearl —
   jin ju, hae ok, ku sul.

How you hide your age
   among the beautiful curls —
the curved glazed ears of seaweed —
   that later translate

the saline of the ocean
   to *hors d'oeurves*, set on
low shin-high tables,
   accompanying liquid

of deep, distilled, toxic-taste.
   Amid hand-made paper-screens,
soft-wood panels, stylised
   Korean *hanguel* calligraphy, and

the live smoke of eucalyptus
   leaves, emerges an aroma,
one that binds our tongues,
   their utterances like

broken words and phrases,
   piecing together, as *haiku;*
live as a nascent pearl —
   fluttering like breathing itself.

Wonju, South Korea

LEDIG NOTES

      1.

The untarred road sweeps its gravel in a rowdy grey arc.
                            It rains, and then stops — the wet
                    glaze mourns for light.
At night, it is freezing — shingles turning into irregular eroded ice-rocks.

But the path diligently details you, alphabetically
from Letter S Road
to the white wedding-cake cottages:
                            Reynolds — Sanford — Ledig.

      2.

In the rooms, nothing can be kept a secret —
                          every move is a mature wooden
                  crunch under my feet,
every word uttered transmits effortlessly to my neighbours —

But still there is talk — rumours about affairs,
        gossip about contracts, pettiness, absences, misplaced politics,
about weight gain and weight loss —
                        about the obsession of not-to-eat more —

      3.

Eat, eat — someone actually eats pages off from my friend's novel —
                vellum surreptitiously ripped,
                      torn mercilessly for pig fodder —
Emma's Luck turned dark in this beautiful bright light of oncoming spring.

                    Everything is severe in this sharp light —
clarity crowding out sight.

As my friend slumps into the white soft sofa —
                    thinking of the disturbing act of pulp,

another friend hums old Hindi film songs in an Iraqi accent

heightening my nostalgia for *attar* — perfumed rose water —
                    its scent defying the storm
                    of pollen count.

Tales from the Town of Widows settle my unrest,
          For Rouenna
                              I write *Memoirs for a Muse*
on *Fundorado Island* trying to find *Henry's Freedom Box* —
                    all these are beautiful
                    escapes of camaraderie.
I know there are "dangers of an imprecise reading"
in *The Sound of Fishsteps*, in subtle serifs of a 'Calligraphy Lesson',
in hearing *Troilus and Cressida* in Lithuanian tongue —
                              but I'm still grateful for
such oblique blessings.

          4.

The tree-trunks, spindly branches
          of yesterday's winter are filling up —
                    parasols of green and colour — hiding the loneliness of
                    their skin.

We work workman-like in isolation,
          only a brief interlude at dinner —

but dinner is not dinner, just a plethora of food left untasted in haste —
most rushing-off to their cubicles
                    before one can digest the aftertaste.

          5.

At Ledig library I read on rattan, the cosy small of the room
surrounded by dark wood, and spines — branded, glue-stamped —
                    stickers of the founder's logo.

But even here, I can hear rumblings from the bowels of the house
                    where linen tumble-dries cotton to its extreme
          tininess —
normal size vests reduce to bikini-bitesize in high heat.

But where is the passion? — Only mechanical heat overheating skin,
          parching the back of my throat.

Gallons of plastic mineral water
 and slathering slapping swathes of Lubriderm
"advanced therapy" — eases things, though only in part —

    6.

I walk through the sculpture park in The Fields everyday
 tracing out different routes every time —
footfalls soft-landing,
confusing the blades to turn against traffic.

The same familiar life-size pieces of art   appear — installed,
uninstalled —
 their perspective, mood, appearance, change every time I visit
 them.

The dead man in the wood always stands upright
 smiles askance, differently —

The endlessly long angular iron-beams shift yellow angles,
 the paint peeling in perfect curls —
an exact algorithm equation controlling its art and weight.

White androgynous face-masks, appear ruddy
and unblanched.

The huge polyethylene sea-shell
 huddles
wing-like in the shape of a cave.

In the bright red silos, empty of their corn, rice and art,
 I hear *New Bamboo* notes —
 its registers soothe my veins —
melodic strains whisper elegantly like memory,
 like fragments from an old letter —
 bird sounds, distant illusions of passing traffic and airplanes,
baritone elegies in haiku.

All these are my constant friends — people come and go —

unlike the large rectangular stainless steel sheet — its bullet holes
remain as a monument, a mirror
 not allowing the weather to tamper

FRACTALS

with it's flawed glittering presence.

                                      I see its alter-ego in the living room —
its negative image exposing a film
                    charred on foam, turning from deep-coal grey
to crimson-black, to black, and back again —

The lake with its moonbeam stepping-stones
                        beckons me to follow her destiny —

I allow myself to be taken in by her radiance —

There is warmth in the coolness there,
                        there is tactility in the vanishing
point,
                        the point is
a pointillist's vision, bullet marked, beautiful —
                                      a deftly deranged love.

Ghent, New York

DISTRACTED GEOGRAPHIES *(extracts)*

GRAVEYARD

The row of
   tall firs

guard life
   against

death,
   fact

from
   secret.

An avenue
   of arched

light —
   its emerald

glow filtering
   through

the matrix
   of branches,

its hypnotic
   marrow —

sucking me into
   its tunnel.

Wading
   through

the semi-
   tropical

green air,
   I stumble

onto an old
   graveyard,

its disused
   space

guarded by
   a wrought-

iron fence
   and lock,

its mettle
   buried

under the
   sanctity

of granite
   and

head-stone.
   Cryptic

nomenclature
   stating

names and
   dates

reveal only
   neutral

mysteries,
   the rest

choose
   to hide

CHURCH NOTES

under brown
   and green

of soil
   and leaves.

The only
   sounds:

the crackle
   of twigs,

hush of a
   freshly-lit

fire,
   the grace

of silent
   breeze,

my feet's
   shuffle,

tin-scratch
   breath of

my frayed
   lungs,

and the
   dead's

living
   heart-beats.

An invisible
   song erupts.

I see myself
   in an

old church,
   where the

remnant tower
   was once

an elegant limb
   in the

structure's
   stone-weary

body. The choir
   picks up.

A swan-graced
   cellist —

her electric
   beauty set

in the pale
   of her youth —

swims in
   to steady

the waves. Her
   angelic

brows dip, as
   her right arm

travelling with
    the bow's polish

makes miniature
    Calder mobiles,

creating gentle
    short-lived

sketches
    in the air,

their impressions
    and

long languid
    lamentations

make her deep-
    oaked cello

breathe heavy,
    resuscitating

the congregated
    air

with secret
    notes

of libation —
    notes that

escaped from
    the hidden

postcard-stack
    I had

hoarded for
    years on end —

not knowing their
    implications,

or their desires.
    Now they

bloomed: magical,
    and perfectly

intoned. I ran
    into the tower's

inner temple.
    There was

no faith left
    in the apse —

only memories
    of slender

fingers stroking
    the cello,

the *chandipaat*
    baritone

invoking the myth
    of verse,

and images,
    scored

and inked
    permanently

by my script's
    roving italics.

MACEDONIAN TRIPTYCH

NIGHT SHOT, KRUSEVO

Night fell gently on Krusevo, and with it came the heavy-set chill. I descended one of the streets — a long stairway — bold granite cut and joined at impossible angles that led to the town centre. All the shops were closed now. Had it not been for the teenagers who gathered in the town square to liven up the weekend, one would almost have mistaken the place for a ghost town.

I walked up and down the many hill paths that knit the town together. I came upon many corners, some that were patios of old forgotten houses. The new ones did not seem to fit the character of the town however hard they tried with modern techniques and technology. At a clearing between two such buildings, the night view of Pelagonia Plains opened up — Prilep and the surrounding villages glittered in incandescent light like a vast shifting swarm of glow-worms. The sky too was very clear and the constellations put up a brave show to compete with the electric stars on the ground.

A shooting star from the middle of the sky scattered westwards before disappearing in a flash. I held its trajectory in my memory and then in my hand, closed my fists, and made a wish, for peace. Somehow one tends to start with the smallest and most recognizable constellations at hand — my immediate family, my best friends and then others.

At a café bar off the town square, my friend Zoran and I sat on two unclaimed chairs around a small round wicker table on the sidewalk. The cold had made everyone huddle indoors, but I could not bear the smoke and crackle of the cacophonous speakers in that room.

Two old linden trees with their canopy of green feathers provided shelter — the unusually intricate weave fanned outwards into a wide deep dome as if it were a living shifting ceiling-fresco, hiding from us the secrets of the sky above. The neon street lamps, the green haze, the mist, the shadow of the church spire — it was a magical mix.

When I ordered brandy, lemon, salt and hot water, the owner-waiter looked totally perplexed at my meek intentions but he complied. Zoran was safe with his request — the fiery local Lozova Rakija. When I told him that the water he brought me was only lukewarm, he told me that his kettle could only heat up to sixty degrees. Somehow this statement seemed to, for a moment, sum up the country's decaying state — potential that it had failed to live up to. Boiling point pegged halfway down the thermometric scale must surely be a sign of cynicism and helplessness, perhaps even hopelessness.

Our chairs were perfectly placed to watch the street life — young women in their tightest best traipsed along dexterously — high heels and the uneven cobbles providing constant tension of stature, shape and gait. The sound of the local disco and DJ boomed across the valley as the folds of the hills tried their best to absorb the onslaught.

From a house close by, a beautiful peach-skinned Macedonian woman strutted out of the front door with her mother sternly inquiring behind her: 'When will you be back home?' 'Seven in the morning,' she replied, walking away without looking back. The young men and women of the town were going to the central square, preening in full flight. The same time-worn courting rituals were enacted — some were successful, others went home disappointed. But the night's hopeful light at least provided them with an escape — fantasy is an important ingredient for survival in these times.

RIVER DRIM, STRUGA

Dawn breaks with the smell of stale popcorn on the beach. Hundreds of crows trying to peel off the last flakes of husk. The water is calm — the calm hiding the mountains that break the horizon. A middle-aged man drifts into the water's frame — his boat sturdy, but the varnish erased by the salt of many seas and seasons. The paddle, a pole reaching the shore's shallows — fresh pickings of leftovers.

The sand looks disturbed from last night's frolic, but the morning rakes the grains back to order.

It is still very calm — the dawn's transparent blue struggles to announce its arrival. By now the boatman has swept across the horizon, his silhouette visible as a mere suggestion.

I walk on to the sand, bare feet craving to meet the beach as it receives my footsteps with caution. I look out towards that infinite line that meets the horizon. The crows, the boatman and the masterful ripples disturb the calm illusion of the scene — a wet canvas — no paint, no rain, no stretched linen — just unbroken light forcing the dawn free from its shackles and this morning's extra-calm confusion.

It is pure as day-starts can be — there is a hint of hope, the still water lulls me even as the adulterous sand draws me to its silicates, making the underside of my feet bleed. I leave a foot trail — the pug-marks tell only part of the story — but that is enough for my own beehive, the sticky cavernous cells ooze passion, blood, and their inherent imagination.

༓

WHITE BOATS, LAKE OHRID

At night, the waters of Ohrid let open the floating white coffins — their hulls scrape the blue-black surface of wet glass-liquid —

allowing me to see history's transparence — this ancient land where King Porus's sailors once blessed the fish.

Empty white boats — their stern bobbing — shake off corpses of the past. But it is so beautiful here; why do I think of this as a tragedy?

Perhaps the pebbles under this coral-blue water map a mosaic — a wet hieroglyphic that predicts my will inked in natural italics —

their colours bleeding the beauty of haunted boats — a fleet docked like a school of crucifix planted upright in a cemetery at night.

White boats have their secrets written in the indelible ink of dark — invisible like the absent white letters cast in grave concrete.

VISITING CAVAFY

For all I did and all I said
let them not search to find who I am
— CONSTANTINE CAVAFY, 'Concealed'

Cavafy, when you called me,
I was afraid to negotiate

the ungeometric alleyways
that led me to your house.

When I finally got there,
you weren't there in sight.

Your rooms vacantly crowded
with words and parchments

of your own prize — your gift
and your love for the sea,

its waves, on which words
themselves rolled, scattering surf.

Out on the streets, when we
walked together singing ballads,

you were only interested
in the Nubian boys you sighted —

their wide beautiful eyes,
their earth-coloured

bodies that shone their youth
in the blinding salt-edged light.

"For all I did and all I said
let them not search to find

who I am." All I care about
is the dark ink that fuelled

your heart, one that invisibly
spilt, when you silently cried.

NILE SONGS ON FELUCCA SAILS

Rhythms of ancient hieroglyphics
   reflect their half-secrets

on linen-stretched sails, full-blown,
   flapping cautiously like the serif

of their own characters — coiled,
   looped, intertwined, geometric —

the labyrinthine history
   unravelling only so much at one time.

Like feluccas — modest, light,
   reliable — they carry history,

writing undeciphered scripts
   mapping the past and present,

entombed on the lap of river Nile.
   Writings that chart moments

of ancient truth and time,
   preserved in the crypts and chambers

buried along the banks
   where soil clashes with silt,

and silt with sand, that eventually
   submits to the heat of the sun.

The currents of the Nile
   change just as unpredictably

as the sand on the dunes,
   a surface that never presents

the same shape or sound.
   Desertscape is meant to be

impermanent — to veil and protect
   the sacredness of preserved life,

tradition and untying time.

ALEXANDRIA

The wide wet corrugated arc
   of the Mediterranean's turquoise
washes Alexandria's shores,
     garnering in its sweep, all the boats
that accidentally gathered
     into a garland of rainbows.

I had once met a poet here —
   who reminisced about youth
and beauty, about sea and heat —
     Cavafy knew full well, the intricate
madness and bacchanalia
     poetry serves up.

Azza and Mostafa listened
   with patience, soaking in
my grief of private losses,
     the unsure damp edges spilling out
onto the ancient banks of this
     aquamarine sun-struck city.

There is something undiscovered
   about this place — its logic,
its overt desire not to adhere.
     Perhaps that is why the city's
sunken library that holds
     a great part of our civilization

remain in my dear friends' custody.
   Their warmth and wisdom, string
together magic beads of an imagined
     necklace, afloat with the basics
of living — a love that allows
     ancient papyrus to unscroll and give.

SHATTERED SHELTERS

The bomb unpeeled taking a long time to unleash,
from the subterranean desert-chambers of secrecy,
   subterfuge and diplomacy.

The fatal slow-release
mechanism shattered every roof in the city,
   spilling sand, coated in musk — mushroom-sanctity —

shrouding the devastation of terraces. These
catacombs — now exposed tiers of asymmetry,
   a matrix of grids and bass-relief — a peculiar beauty

of deconstruction. From high above, the unease
of uneven squares and roofs, resembled uncannily —
   vulture-pecked carcasses devoured greedily

in haste. Inside, men and women lay asleep,
anointed in gunpowder and rubble, permanently
   frozen in wasted blood, charred unsystematically

in precise poetic detonation.

NOTE: The catacombs of Kom ash-Shuqqafa in Alexandria is the largest known Roman burial site in Egypt, discovered accidentally in 1900 when a donkey-cart fell through part of the roof. The *abb abb* ... rhyme-scheme reflects the actual three-tiered construction of the site itself.

ELECTRIC TEXT
for Seamus Heaney

... O that awful deep down torrent O and ...
... the sea the sea crimson something like fire ...
—JAMES JOYCE, *Ulysses*

On the dark dank of Dublin's quayside walls,
    neon-text flash poetry —

damp concrete iambs ring and meld —
    voltage melting water into fire.

Electric-pink blossoms in the heat
    and scent of its own blush,

extracting every photon of its crimson essence.
    Wrought-iron curves of the Ha'penny arch

span the wet-shimmerings of Liffey,
    metallic strength commit torque —

enjambments refuse to be contained in
    the slanted embankments of these unsure times.

It is winter's first night —
    the air flakes open their crystals

chilling my unprepared body, tempting
    its tissues to willingly crack open,

leaving my own vulnerability bare.
    Here, the only truth is the text itself —

its ambition, its fluorescent intent, its illusion,
    and its sententious stream to the sea.

SEARCHING FOR SEAMUS

... in a warm July you lay
Christened and smiling ...
While I, a guest in your green court,
At a west window sat and wrote ...
— S. H., 'A Peacock's Feather'

1. MARYLAND, USA | 1989

    When I first saw you —
I was a mere face

    in a word-rapt audience —
while you, on stage,

    constructed lyrics,
letting the tip of your tongue

    and silver-white hair
tremble in the perfect tenor

    of its substance,
a fluid frequency

    that even a tested equation
found hard to balance.

    Eccentricity has its gifts,
its genius containing

    its own sanity and calm.
The Haw Lantern opened

    its jaws — the title
page pronouncing your space

    and inviting my deep want
of your ink — the sepia-scribbled

    "as I pass (p.39)"
celebrating with

the peacock's rain-dance,
my own country's pride.

2. DUBLIN, IRELAND | 1997

Today in Sandymount
I looked for you, as you did

for your *father's ashplant*
many years ago.

I don't know why I went
on this search

knowing full well
you weren't there,

but elsewhere gracing a shoot
"plunging through glar

and Glitty Sheughs".
But the script for me

remains unfinished ...
the dotted line of words,

of memory, of epiphany,
is something I know

tide won't wash away.
The secret lies

in accepting word's own
intent, one that scripts

one's own fate, with its
desire, fatality,

unpredictability,
and its elocuted magic.

CHANGING HANDS

The lone lighthouse coated in salt
    and sun-white enamel, looked uncomfortable

at the edge of the silent north Irish Sea.
    Donaghadee demanded to be noticed

in this holiday-perfect light, as crowds
    flocked like untrained geese to see

the maritime mysteries of this tower's fate.
    The wood in *Woodview* — my friend's house —

would soon be stripped off its old badge,
    its lacquer and paint burnt off

to make space for new occupants,
    their wealth hoarded up in the attic-space.

My pewter hip-flask which weathered
    relentless battering of a previous owner,

was further battered in the electric steam
    of boiling heat, and then frozen overnight.

Any life that might have had ambition
    to live, perished in this pressure.

The flask's silver state changed shape —
    an intimation of what it may contain.

Bushmill's fluid age was hardier
    than it appeared, its pungent peat

fermenting gently, helping clear the weeds
    among the garden's vine-twisted trellises.

Even the medieval sun-dial peering out
    of the over-growth found it difficult

to tell time — its own pewter strength
    weathered all the neglect with compassion,

its chronographic gradations providing
    more time than the day can normally

hold. This house — its surprising
    arches, slates, and wild iridescent

colours — awaited our unplanned ceremony.
    We stepped into its precincts

holding the luck and charm
    of a rescued treasure — its ancient preserved

libation and our unexpected touch
    providing quiet grace and baptism —

carrying the first blessing: an unposted letter
    from an unborn child.

❦

GUINNESS
for Derek Walcott

    The 'dark sleep' beer seeps in
gently into the mind's crevice,
    dulling the nerves, sparking

    a lightness in the blood-stream
that quickens the corpuscle-flow.
    The head gathers froth, cream

    simmers in chilling
particles, swirling in gentle loops
    as it descends to the cunning

    bottom of the glass' wide curve
and transparency. Here,
    deep in its belly, it curls,

    threatens to roar, the flow
of an unknown sound, incipient
    rumblings of a liquid volcano.

BALLYNAHINCH

Irish liquid destroyed shamrock's imperial illusion
  of green to the (un)royal blue, healthy blues

that confirmed the green comfort of health —
  tropical green like sanitised salad

with the best of sprouted intention —
  vegetables roasted to their toasted civility.

Fish dropped their fins and willingly shed
  their bone and spine, to accommodate

the juice of their finless grace,
  and the squid's unscripted ink.

Belfast was grey, cold as neglected gold —
  an accidental lack of mineral knowledge.

The sea — its stony borders and forgotten niches —
  lent humour – its memory keeping everything alive.

The house kept its hand-built dignity, its prized
  unsold open spaces, its tactile humanness —

the rest was commerce, speculation,
  sentimentality. What mattered

was hope and its inherent dreams,
  dreams that allow one to dream on, and live.

THE WAILING WALL
for Yehuda Amichai

Glazed off-white floors
    polished by pilgrim's feet

reflect rugged roughness of
    The Wailing Wall —

its niches preserving
    memories and secrets,

scripted on scrolls of paper,
    cloth and cardboard,

installed and re-installed
    every second

by many different hands.
    Men and women

in two unequally
    divided enclosures, pray

with quiet and equal zeal.
    On the other side,

this very wall
    preserves the sanctity

of another faith
    in the Dome of the Rock,

divided and shared,
    cemented by the joins

of the same Jerusalem stone.

Jerusalem, 1997

THE WAILING WALL, REVISITED

*A human being
is not symmetrical.*
— SRECKO KOSOVEL

1.

I gently touch you now
   not the way I did
eleven years ago —

not with that yearning
   for faith and peace,
but with a private prayer

for inner calm, care,
   stillness; and
for forgiveness and love.

The gleaming hand-worn
   shine on Jerusalem stone,
where the public merges

with the private,
   where prayer and passion
collide and unite —

where a certain kind
   of kindness changes
to another kind —

where a certain kind
   of passion changes
to another kind

of desire. It is
   a blessing of time —
eleven years is a lifetime.

2.

As I try once again
    to wedge in
a piece of coded-paper

into the cracks
    and joins of The Wall,
I discover

another paper
    behind the new one
resisting my approach.

I try to force it in —
    the more I try
the more impossible it gets.

Failing, I now try to
    take out the old paper
that prevents my will,

take out that piece
    and resize
my own new prayers —

but the longing
    of past years resists
dislodging the old.

I prise out
    the old folded sheet —
it looks weathered

and yellow
    like the local stone's
sun-stained ochre.

I open it —
    it is the same one
I had put in

eleven years ago.
    Time had preserved
memory,

preserved my wishes.
    Was I the same then
as I am now?

Was the feeling then
    more sincere
than now?

Passion for life
    never wanes for some.
New love

like old love
    balances
its inherent truths.

3.

Here, gun-slung soldiers,
    pilgrims, children,
and men in black garb —

move forwards
    and backwards —
their axis, their waist —

a symmetry
    that instils and heightens
their own faith —

a symmetry
    I cannot hope
to aspire to,

as I am —
    like Kosovel's man —
not symmetrical.

Jerusalem, 2008

DESERT TRIPTYCH

SPRING IN THE DESERT I

The pointillist's
  shepardic spray
of lemon and mustard

  on the pale-
green shrubbery,
  appear and disappear

just as the yellow
  sun's nascent
fluctuating heat.

Meron Valley, Galilee

🌱

SPRING IN THE DESERT II

Off-white parasols
  of fine lace,
veil the transient green

  of this desert spring.
Brief as it may be,
  the petals guard

this new bride, with
  the illusion and fantasy
of the season's passion.

Nazareth

🌱

SPRING IN THE DESERT III

    These tiny flowers
like miniature *menorahs*
    light the candelabra,

and the *ethrons*
    whose sharp citrus taste
bless the *lular:*

    the palm branch,
wetting its serrated,
    gorged, enticing tip.

Megiddo

🌿

DIASPORA

    I walk with
        the travelling text —

        the wandering Jew —
as history's space

    remain codified
like the image itself.

    I feel I am
in a watchmaker's den,

    in a room
full of clocks

    out of sync.
A forest of projectors

    show slides,
a whirlwind of frames,

    a mechanised groan
grown accustomed

    to the calamity
of confusion.

    In this winding
shapeless tunnel,

    I feel at-home
in the black

    and in sparse light.
Here, nobody

    recognises my pen,
but my metaphors

are impregnated
on the grey and white

walls
as I walk

with my own scroll,
travelling

with personal
texts — Hebraic,

elegaic, hidden,
and ungathered.

*Diaspora Museum,
Tel Aviv*

🌱

AT PESTO CAFE

Smoke hangs
   surreptitiously,

undecided
   whether to hide

the poet's mike
   and throat,

the Heinekien
   poster, or

the Hebrew
   text's dactyls.

Khan Hall, Jerusalem

CARVING SALMON

The besotted fish,
    finless in its flight,
stares dead straight

    at Mount Zion,
from the ochre stone's
    unsure solidness.

The waterless valley
    dips between
Mishkenot Sha'ananim

    and The Old City
inviting us
    to swim through

the unsure tide
    and times,
time that ticks

    in uneasy peace,
just like the peace
    destroyed by pieces

of broken fins,
    arrows, missiles,
bones, and fate.

Cinematheque Restaurant,
Jerusalem

ISRAELI AIRWAVES

    Like omnipresent
grasshoppers,

    everyone here
has sprouted

    antennaes,
like Herod's ears.

    Misnamed 'mango',
these miniature horns

    pop up with
unsuspecting rings —

    unintelligent
communication —

    leaving this land
immobilised.

Jaffa

CIRCUMCISION

Inside the white-washed
    purity
of a Bet Shemesh
    bomb-shelter,

blood spills
    relentlessly —
a baby's howl
    is religiously

drowned
    in prayer's
organisation
    and confusion.

A small twist
    of a knife
and shield make
    stainless-steel stains

on tender skin's
    innocence,
branding young
    flesh with law —

Judaic solemnity.
    What law is this
that preaches
    humanity with blood?

What logic is this
    that uses
nuclear shelter
    as synagogue

to preach peace?
    The chants grow
louder, frenetic,
    drowning out

echoes of abortion
    and holocaust,
to celebrate life
    that bleeds crimson —

juice's sanctity,
    that circumscribes
text
    of promised lives.

The baby now sleeps
    in silenced pain
amid the unforgiving
    joy of religion,

among believers
    who stand sheathed
unwilling
    to accomodate

by-standers
    of other faith,
inspite of
    their skull-

capped presence.
    For me,
only one thing
    matters:

the love
    of the child, born
in innocence
    and peace.

Bet Shemesh

ALMAYA, JAFFA

I like to keep my doors open —
It is like sitting in the desert —

Under studio's arched ceiling flutes,
roof-paint uncoats, peeling lime white.
Reverberating invisible sounds —
oud and violin, and a lone desert voice.

Outside, the sea picks up its waves
in harmony. Inside, there are red
oriental rugs, an uncleared stage
with notes from a concert past,

kettle for sage tea, Iraqi sweets,
bottles of various shapes, and chairs —
lots of mismatched chairs
like relatives from different tribes.

I like to keep my doors open —
It is like sitting in the desert —

'Two flaming loves can burn you,'
you say. A Japanese girl
who once heard you at a WOMAD
concert in Australia stumbles

past your door, then stops
to look inside. 'Is that you —
the one in the poster on your door',
she asks. You nod humbly

in your oblique quiet way.
'Almaya' — the name of your space —
is christened then — 'the universe
that embraces the waters'.

I like to keep my doors open —
It is like sitting in the desert —

The calm of the desert,
the turbulence of the sea,
  the early whistling of winds
before a gathering storm,

  the Bedouin's elongated cry,
the brothers' lisping embrace,
  hand-woven cream pashmina
shawl — all score, the elements.

I like to keep my doors open —
It is like sitting in the desert —

READING WITH THE WIND

    Reading in the firm wind
pitted aginst elements,

    I graciously
allowed nature to win,

    and let the wind carry my words
into the clean war-stricken air.

    The irony contained
in the golden beauty of the

    Dome of the Rock
and the free openness of

    Notre Dame terrace, wavered
in its own atomic weight.

    The microphone's static tried
to balance the equation,

    but how can you think of balance
when you stand so high

on the seam of Jerusalem's
    East-West divide, far from gravity,

    on this earth's fault-lines?
The wind roars

    and then decides to caress
my lips, maybe to allow

    a few words of kindness
to be uttered, somewhat safely.

On the Roof of Notre Dame, Jerusalem

10.
PRAYER CALL

*God spoke once in the dark: dead sound
in the dead silence. I turned / in my sleep. // ....
Suspended on cold iron, branded on air.*
— YVOR WINTERS, 'The Precision'

PRAYER CALL: HEAT

I wake cold, I who
Prospered through dreams of heat
Wake to their residue,
Sweat, and a clinging sheet.
—THOM GUNN, 'The Man with Night Sweats'

Outside, "Allah-u-Akbar"
    pierces the dawn air —
It is still dark.

Inside, electric light
    powers strength
to my feverish body.

Mosque minaret
    radiate prayer-calls
all around —

like coded signals
    emanating
from old radio

transmitter-towers —
    relaying the dangers
of heat in this stale air.

༄

A bare body
    sleeps peacefully
beside me —

her face's innocence,
    and generous curve
of her eye-lashes

try to sweep
    away my
skin's excess heat,

one that is fast
    making my bones
pale and brittle.

❦

A brief lull
    lingers outside.
I cannot hear

the heavy lyrics,
    their rhymes
trying to invoke

peace and respect,
    their wafting baritone
instilling faith.

Such things
    are luxuries
for me now.

I lie, trying
    to piece together
the eccentric song

of my own
    inadequate breathing.
It is a struggle.

❦

It is also a mystery.
    Mystery of a body's
architecture,

its vulnerability,
    its efficient circulation —
they are perfect

models I remember
    from school's
very early lessons.

They are only
    how things ought to be,
not how they are.

❦

Only now, I realise
    the intent
of prayer's persuasion,

its seductive expression.
    I also value
the presence and grace

of the body that willingly
    lies next to me,
as her breath

tries to realign my will's
    magnetic imprint, and
my heart's irregular beat.

My vision is awash
    with salt
of her night-sweat.

My hearing trapped —
    within eardrum's
circuitous drone —

in Arabic's passion,
    the ink
of its parabolic script —

sung loud
    so that no
slant or serif

can be erased,
    altered
or misunderstood.

❦

Religion's veil
    and chiffon —
its sheer black

and translucence,
    its own desire
to give and want,

its ambition
    to control
and preserve.

Such songs
    mean nothing
to me

if one's own
    peace and privacy
remain unprotected,

or, are not at ease.
    I want
the chant's passion,

its heat
    to settle
my restlessness.

I want the song
    to soothe
my nerve-ends

so that the pain
    subsides
and faith's will

is able to rise.
    I also want
the beauty

of this faith
    to raise
its heat —

not body-heat —
 but the heat
of healing.

❧

But for now,
 the diaphanous lull
is a big boon.

Here, I can calculate
 the exact path
of my body's

blood-flow,
 its unpredictable
rise and fall

of heat, and
 the way it infects
my imagination.

❧

I step out
 of the room's
warm safety.

I see
 the morning light
struggling

to gather muscle
 to remove
night's cataract.

❧

Again,
 the mosques threaten
to peel

their well-intentioned
    sounds —
to appease us all.

But I see
    only darkness,
and admire it —

I also admire
    the dignity and gravity
of heavy-water

and its blood —
    its peculiar
viscous fragility,

its own struggle
    to flow,
sculpt and resuscitate.

❧

In quiet's privacy,
    I find
cold warmth

in my skin's
    permanent sweat,
in its acrid edge,

and in my own
    god's
prayer-call.

❧

EATING RICE & FISH

Maachey Bhaatey Bangaale
— AN OLD BENGALI SAYING

1. RICE

Delicately sheathed,
    wrapped
in papery husk —

I love the feel and
    elegance of long slender
rice grains —

their seduction
    and charm,
their aroma and shape —

their fine flavour
    and
the deep virgin taste.

2. FISH

I use my finger-tips
    to pry open,
feel, and sense

the hidden taste
    of fish —
its flesh and scales,

its coarseness
    and gloss,
its geometry,

its muscle-bone
    and tone —
Gently, I relish it all.

ARIA'S FOOTPRINT

The block of text
   I tirelessly worked on,

refused to resolve
   its intent.

Then you came along —
   your new body —

new fingers, new feet —
   tracing their outline

on white margin-spaces
   of my unruled page.

Ink-edges marked
   your new step

like miniature ice-bergs
   refusing to melt,

lest this archipelago's
   map

altered the safety
   of currents.

I stared
   at the unfinished

silhouette
 and its soft edges —

its subtle tentative
   frankness,

its clear honesty
   of ambition,

its deep sepia-tinged
    maturity.

I retraced
    its periphery —

one that would
    expand

the grip's strength
    in time,

each digit adding up
    to an equation

no human can balance.
    My son's first

footprint on paper —
    stamping a new will —

a new score's
    untrained future,

and the miracle
    of *tabula rasa*.

BOWL

The cracked bowl that I mean to repair everyday
keeps getting neglected by my secret awe for bone china
        and its story of unbreaking.

There were happier times when it stood perfect
in its shape, its porcelain clay-fluted nape
        elegant as a swan's neck.

I found it in a heap of beautiful pottery,
one among many, that its maker carefully crafted
        in her tropical rooftop studio.

To me it was new even after it accidentally
slipped from my hands as I tried to wipe
        the Delhi dust

that clung to us like camel-brown film,
like innocuous powder — transparent and deceptive
        like make-up.

There are scenes I painted on its milk-white skin,
words I wrote, lines etched in, fragments of poems
        left unfinished, hieroglyphic

encoded secrets
that only I knew and understood,
        impervious to gossip's glare and jealous chatter.

Today, I shall bring out Super Glue
and try to make repairs.
        Maybe I will splurge

on a rare metal —
silver or even gold, to seal the cracks and fill them
        with molten healing.

Anointing it with gold,
memory, love and desire,
    is better than the perfection

of its prior shape. Unbroken, poised as it was,
unhurt love is not necessarily purer
    than love that is flawed.

Kintsukuroi is a prayer I have been granted.
My bowl deserves the lacquer touch of a silver-wish
    and the purest of rare gold.

---

* Kintsukuroi (n.) (v. phr.) "to repair with gold"; the art of repairing pottery with gold or silver lacquer and understanding that the piece is more beautiful for having been broken.

STRIKING MATCHES

1. LABORATORY

An upturned ship,
   July's red sky —
logo's brand equity —

crimson waiting
   to be fired.
The narrow parallel

sides, diamond-etched,
   bit-mapped — codes
that deceive history —

phosphorescence,
   each packed close
together,

awaiting the strike-
   burn, poised
for life, to ignite.

2. BOMBAY | MUMBAI

You arranged
   for many of us
to meet,

but only
   the die-hards
turned up

soaked in ink-dye
   and sweat, disgusted
and derailed. Only

politics and poverty
   can power this city,
you remarked.

But there was love
   inspite of this
meagre gathering.

3. NEW DELHI

I grope around
 blinded by the power-
cut. I look

for just the basics.
 A half-burnt candle,
its wax still warm

from recent use,
 scars my fingers.
But such sacrifices

are commonplace.
 A match-stick
is the only hope.

4. HOSPITAL

Sun's edges are dark,
 so are my heart's.
No amount of air

will light it up.
 My nurse's misguided
flames, spark.

5. AFTER-BURNS

Wood-tip, bulbous,
 stares
in heat, frustrated.

No sparring partner
 in sight.
Pulp and chemical

set, married to burn:
 a relationship
I can live with.

There is a deceptive
 glow
on my cheeks.

NECK[LACE]

Glowering, crystal-white pearls — soon-to-be stained.
        The ends of her necklace are unclasped at my will
and I need the pearls to slide off their string —

They fall on the cold white floor
        scattering randomly —
most of them split apart in imperfect hemispheres —
        their raw insides aching for polish —

I mix black and red ink
        using my bruised finger-tips.
The creases of my palms and fingers,
        the skin underneath my nails,
        and my hand's sweat pores are all drenched —
soaked in dark wine-red mist
        as if my bloodied hands
tried to dry off the excess liquid
in hot coal-dust —

Cracked pearls —
        open split-atoms —
virgin lace-white soaked in menstrual flow —
        beauty-body, desire-sex,
the exotic—all chained as the pearl necklace once was.

Crystal glimmer —
        the inner light from the pearls own womb
struggling to seek out
        what lies beyond its shell,
            beyond the smooth skin of her neck,
beyond the soft smell of her sex —

Large tear-drops roll off her eyes —
        the salt mixes with the pearls' red stain —
        a sudden gasp of steam coughs up
as if salt and pearls were not meant to meet or react,
        not remembering how inextricably
they were once linked under the deep saline ocean —

   Sadness-preciousness, anger-hurt —
how these seemingly innocuous pearls peel such emotion.
  I pick up the disengaged pearls off the floor,
try to lick clean and taste their blood and salt —
    they glower, glow — glazed —
still wanting more,
much more of the essentials and the insatiables.

🌱

NOVÆMBER

The constellation burned
 furiously this month

as the Nova ended in
 a trail of fire, spilling

meteorites toward us
 laced in magnetic flux

 like a coughing cobra
hissing with excess venom. The

 meteors splitting like genes,
chromosomes dividing, rebuilding

 matter as the cosmic
conflagration traced an orbit

of space, of the sun and the storm
 that welded each month

with the other
 in a cyclical calendar,

fused in the mire
 of earth, water, and frozen fire.

SAHARA

Sand feels like water,
    a perennial thaw under my feet.
Bare foot, I climb the sands
    that slope nonchalantly
for miles — undulating dunes
    lit to absolute blinding starkness
by the clarity of sun's shear.
    Sky's sheer pure-blue off-sets
the crest-line of dune-ridges,
    their changeable sharp-edged arcs.

Upon looking closely
    against this azure palette,
I see a continuous stream
    of dust, sand blowing off the crests,
scraping off the powder, grain by
    grain, delicately, as if by an artist —
final sandpaper finish depending
    on the dance of the wind itself.
But nothing is final or permanent
    Here — these slow-moving waves

form temporary ridges —
    each one different in pattern,
each with a unique gene-imprint.
    I stand on one of the crests,
my feet straddling dune's dual slopes,
    sunk in sand, millions of quartzite —
lit, unlit, warm, frozen.
    I try to walk on this wind-swept
Terrain — sand feels like water —
    sensuous sheets of tingle,

not water-wet but fluid-like,
    water that is sand —
hot, grainy, chilly, powdery,
    all at the same time.
My feet sink, buried further.
    I feel the increasing depth

more than before — sand feels
   like water, water sand —
sand, paper-thin and gossamer-strung —
   a camel-coloured canvas,

a quilt cloaking the Tunisian desert —
   waiting generously for new cuts,
acts of passion, daring, and chisel.

❧

MIRRORWORK

Untutored sparks, broken and oblique like flirting
   glitters, shoot out of the *ghagra* that surrounds

her hips, her thighs, and her small ankles.
   The skirt, intimate and natural, woven insane

with raw cotton colours, bright and enthusiastic,
   like an October-burst of late autumn.

Colours spilling from and into every crack,
   every crevice, every fissure of the fabric

that caresses and smoothes her olive skin.
   She wears them all with the mystery

of a rainbow, here one moment, gone another.
   Quiet pastels of evanescence warm her body,

teasing the spaces and the air that circulate
   between woven threads and the invisible hair

on her lava-smooth skin, veiled
   to the outside, only to refract,

surreptitiously like a charged coy lover,
   reflecting unsuspecting embroidered rounds —

the mirrorwork — that embraces her skirt, her shirt,
   her dance, and her bosom's intimate breathings.

OFFERING

the kindness of libation, lyric, and blood

her endless notes left for me —
                        little secrets, graces —
        trills recorded on blue and purple parchment
to be lipped, tasted, devoured —

only the essence remains —
        its stickiness, its juice, its memory

seamless juxtaposition —
        the brute and the passion,
                dry of the bone and wet of the sea,
coarseness of the page and smooth of the nib's iridium

I try and trace a line, a very long line —

        the ink blots
                as this line's linear edge
dissolves and frays —

like capillary threads
        gone mad
                twirling in the deep heat of the tropics —

threads unravelling,
        each sinew tense with the want of moisture
and the other's flesh

there are no endings here —
only beginnings —
                        precious incipience —

translucent drops of sweat
        perched precariously on her collar-bone
                      waiting to slide,
roll unannounced into the gulleys
that yearn to soak in the rain —

heart-beat shift
the shape of globules
         as they alter their balance and colour,
changing their very point of gravity —

constantly deceiving the other

I stand, wanting —
         wanting more of the bone's dry edge,
the infinite blur of desire,
                           the dream,
       the wet, the salt, the ink,
and   the underside of her skin

❦

FEBRUARY: 28¼

February has fewer
days than the other months; therefore it is more cruel
than the rest.
— JOSEPH BRODSKY, *Tsushima Screen 1978*

   The moon takes as many days
to circle the earth, as the second month takes

   to survive, lasting out, just over
four weeks of breathing each year.

   The month of February, living for the briefest
time, is only allowed to contain the fewest

   days, a peculiar grace granted by the
ancient almanacs. Toiling, even though

   every four years it manages to pull together
the extra day with the accumulated quarters,

   it's barely enough for a leap. With fewer days,
it is more cruel than the rest,

   even more so than April, though, the child born
on the twenty-ninth is blessed to be forever young.

HEAT

It is early in the season — the mere beginning of summer. But everywhere, it is searing hot. Heat melts everything, even metal — burns wood, tissues, and human heart.

Stones on the ground steam, simmer, ignite — the tarmac slow-melts into viscous black sea.

Neem tree branches in front of my study shrink like emaciated skeletal, architecture of apocalyptic shape — a haze, blanched wood-green, etiolated.

The power lines spark — no power for hours on end. Every day it is the same.

Telephone lines stutter in their speech — a new language of inconsequence.

Even clock hands find it hard to move — keeping time is unnatural in these times.

Tap water scalds everything that it falls on — turning all furnace hot.

Heat rises from everything — surfaces, terraces, walls, linen, food, water — everything is vaporous.

A mirage shimmering, a hallucinatory vacuum, a red-hot deception.

Eyes are mere sockets, human skin rough leather, and tongue a shriveled dry prune.

No moisture, just steam, heat, heat, and more heat. Barren. Everything seems in short supply, except heat.

Summer 2014

11.
FACSIMILE

*When love on stilts
picks its way along gravel paths
and reaches the treetops
I too in cherries would like
to experience cherries as cherries,....*
— GÜNTER GRASS, 'Cherries'

*The polyp that insinuates
inky tentacles between the rocks
can make use of you. You belong to him //
and don't know it. You're he and you think you're you.*
— EUGENIO MONTALE, 'Indian Serenade'

LIGHT IN MY STUDY

I am blessed with light
    naturally granted:
pure, unhindered,
    accommodating, peaceful.
On the greyest of days,
    its invisible rainbow
brightens the grain of walls
    that reflect the true tenor
of emotion, its compressed
    colours giving warmth
that only pure whiteness
    can hope to contain.

Today, the light streaks in,
    peeling the old skin off
my body, making me bare
    to its resonant heat.
I catch a slice of its rays,
    try to cut a piece and hide
it for some other dark time.
    But my secret storage fails,
as it spills and leaks,
    trying to be uncontained,
as light's insatiable desire
    is to plasmaically spread,
and escape.

SUN-BLANCHED BLOOD

1.

It is mid-afternoon now,
    the sun streaks slant wards

through the attic's double-glazing
    melting the scorched ink

in my crowded note-book
    that lies blanched

on the sparse weathered table.
    Hardened sepia-stained lines

that once approximated to
    a flock of metaphors,

now rearrange themselves
    into a congregation of phrases,

a lineation of new line-breaks:
    stops that defy

even the physics of refraction,
    thoughts that now re-surface

and resurrect just as
    passion and reverence did

within the folds of *The Prophet*.

2.

    It is still mid-afternoon,
the blue blaze makes the pages

    of my book flip over gently
in the invisible wind of silence.

The heat penetrating the glass
focuses even more fiercely

    smoking out redolent similes,
questioning the whole point,

    the nib of writing itself.
Underneath the permanent scar

    of jet-black fluid and heat
is pulp, half-dead.

    Beneath the persistent hoarse-
drone of metal-scratching

    is bleached pulp, half-alive,
its cotton laid sheets

    carefully encoded with
the magic arc of a gold-tip.

    Words appear, and more
words. And under them all,

    I discover much later,
a small spring insect

    that lay mummified,
quietly crushed below

    the weight of words,
its innocence and juice

    trapped under oppression
of ambition and intellect,

    baptised and bloodied.

3.

It is mid-afternoon,
    and I too lie, dead-

still, blanched, bloodied.

EATING GUAVAS OUTSIDE TAJ MAHAL

The heavy drunken aroma
   of fresh guavas
is too sweet for me to bear.

Instead, I drink its nectar
   not as liquid-pulp
but as raw unsmooth fruit.

I bite its light-green rough skin
   the way I used to
approach a sugarcane stalk

as a child
   crunching every fibre
to extract their juice.

There are memories —
   memories attached to food
and their consumption.

There are memories
   about the rituals of intake —
how certain foods

are allowed or disallowed
   depending on God's stance
and their place

in the lofty hierarchies
   they create.
How misplaced these stations

are — God, Emperor, Man
   all mistaken — proud errors
of selfhood, status, and ego.

Even under prayer's veil,
   there is something about
eating guavas with unwashed

hands, tasting their taste before
   masala, lemon and rock-salt
turn them into sprightly salad —

seed's bone-crack intentions
   slip, cloaked —
buried before they fruit.

🦗

DIALOGUE | CRICKET

   I write, you write,
you speak, I respond;
   my response sparks
another in you.
   Your speech bowls
an out-swinger.
   I leave it,
graciously
   for the keeper
of words.
   I bat through
the sessions,
   all day.
Next morning,
   century-struck
from the evening
   before, I open
with flashy
   drives and
deft glances;
   then I declare.
You script an epic
   in reply,
full of monumental
   highs, and hardly
any lows.
   The score-line
strikes up
   another jazz tune,
calypso dubbing
   text after text.

Then comes
    the slower
ball,
    bowled
with a deception
    that completely
catches us out,
    in a loop
that includes
    only city cliques.
But their dialogue
    is only heard
in limited circles,
    diffused as quickly
as their
    cigarette smoke.
Our words are heard
    by the sky
as it rains,
    not because we
meant it to be so,
    but outpour
and fair play
    are natural course
for our game.
    Yesterday, I watched
a television replay:
    Lara and Tendulkar
in full display.
    What struck me
was not their strokes,
    but their small,
shared
    height of humility.
The TV-clip was
    cut short by
your telephone call,
    a fax
that had travelled
    across the Atlantic
just began to emerge,
    mapping
the game's journey,
    in other words.

12.
ELEGIES

*And even my lament
turns into a paean before my disconsolate heart.*
— RAINER MARIA RILKE, from *Duino Elegies*

*Death, the best of all mysteries, layer
After layer is peeled off your secrecy
Until all that is left is an inexplicable ooze.*
— DOUGLAS DUNN, 'Supreme Death'

DADU

Three years back I held Dadu, my grandfather, through
    the second attack in the Intensive Care Unit,
surrounded by smells of doctors, dis-
    infectants, drugs, and his sweat,
as he convulsed fiercely fighting for life.

I held him all the way through,
    watching the beads of his sweat
glisten among the neon-lit
    panels, pipes, pins, graphs, glucose,
as he cried out breathlessly for life.

The dreaded moments, struggling, gasping to
    live. I was just as drenched as he was. I saw:
His eyes closed, he lay there silently with his
    heaving chest rising and falling
as the sweat beads rolled down his sides.

He breathed back, barely, to
    yet another survival.
I was not present there, this
    time. Trying to hold him again
from ten thousand miles

away, I overheard by mail: Didu,
    my grandmother, absolutely cold, choked, pale,
spoke the only words she's spoken since,
    "All our grandchildren except you saw him,
you weren't here, to save him, this time."

SUSPENDED PARTICLES
i.m. Jacqueline Bardolph

Two shafts
   of sunlight

bisect
   this room —

this
   well-defined

twin-track
   of silver-dust,

floats,
   suspended

in the dense
   still air.

Outside,
   the traffic roars,

inside,
   the clock ticks

with well-
   intentioned

regularity,
   quite unlike

the random
   particles

that swim
   aimlessly

in slanted clear-
   cut columns.

A lost bee
   drones in

through
   the window

carelessly
   left ajar

to entertain
   this show,

its minute
   sting

picking
   every particle

it catches
   in its path,

as its
   translucent wings

caught against
   this light,

filter
   specifics

from randomness,
   to make sense

of it all.
   My own sight

trapped within
   my heavy eyelids,

                detects   light pales,
                    the subtle beauty   congregations

                of frenetic   of silver-
                    atoms,   specks

                the nuclear   make themselves
                    weight   invisible,

                weightless   even though
                    as air in space,   their presence

                light as post-   remains,
                    monsoon breeze.   alive

                But as the   and
                    evening-   whispered.

DURING THE STREET PLAY

   In the cobbled quadrangle
rises a primitive voice:

   clear, and elemental.
His figure, draped in raw linen,

   carrying a staff.
Others, black-robed, masked,

   gradually close in
in concentric circles,

   repeating after him the lines
in a choral refrain.

   He is not Moses
the shepherd from Egypt,

he is not even a politician
campaigning for the next season.

He is, perhaps, just a local
student, armed with pamphlets,

leaflets with lines
seeking the rights of humans,

maybe even a little justice.
The stage, very simple.

A quadrangle, this time,
but it could be

a market-place next time,
a street corner, a college campus.

The street-lamps spotlight the act,
or the sun will do if it is day.

The daily-wear is a fine costume,
the play quite straight-forward,

about you, and us,
about now, and in real time.

But that is too much
for the state.

Soon the police arrive,
dismantle the props, oust

the actors, as they exit
protesting in words.

NOTE: Safdar Hashmi, the political playwright, was killed on the streets of New Delhi in 1989 by state agents while performing his play, *Hulla Bol [Let the Noise Speak]*.

GAZA

Soaked in blood, children,
 their heads blown out
even before they are formed.

Gauze, gauze, more gauze —
 interminable lengths
not long enough to soak

all the blood in Gaza.
 A river of blood flowing,
flooding the desert sands

with incarnadine hate.
 An endless lava stream
on a parched-orphaned land,

bombed every five minutes
 to strip Gaza of whatever
is left of the Gaza strip.

Tiny lives snuffed out,
 faces defaced, eyes vacant —
a new holocaust continues

unabated. The world weeps
 red, mourning —
an unceasing blood-song.

2014

MH-17 CRASH

 weightless like air,
lifeless like flotsam —

  lives, fragile — gone.

flesh can't survive
 hate's missile strike.

2014

ELEGY FOR DELHI: 29/10

1.

Dead bodies lay, ripe-pink, charred,
a place I usually find ripe fruits on another day —

pairs of plastic sandals, molten, overturned —
tattered linen smell wet ash — carts, goods, strewn about.

Another day here amid the jostle,
it's hard to steer or park my own shuffle —

but today, there is an awkward flurry of feet —
Diwali and Eid, only a few days away.

Tonight, only smell of burn, blood and despair —
Govindpuri market, bustling, bustling with agony.

A small boy screaming, searching his father's name —
a little girl quietly weeping on the curb side —

others, running around helplessly —
there is din, dust, death — and no light.

2.

Two other blasts in my city — Sarojini Nagar, Paharganj —
places I know well, places I could have been.

There is too much anger, misplaced anger, in people —
these flames that burn do not contain their own anger,

their wild tongues merely sign of others' anger.
No equality in this world, there can ever be —

no amount of praying would solve this heat —
there is din, dust, death — and no light.

3.

I go to the small boy to pretend I am his lost father,
but he does not recognise me —

I sit next to the little girl and cry —
but our tears do not replace the blood or hatred.

There is only chaos, darkness, dust, and death here —
I pray for light, I pray for life —

pray in futility — hoping for compassion, for sanity. But
there is only din, dust, death — and no light.

BABA | FATHER
[S<small>ATYABRATA</small> S<small>EN</small> 23.11.1930 – 14.12.2011]
for Ma

Your ashes have now been scattered
   on River Yamuna's lap —
Ganga's own having accepted
   one of her son's back, weeps.
But the fire within me, still burns.

   As I tentatively walk back up
the steep steps of the Kalindi Kunj ghats
   in the deep dark invisibility
of a December Delhi fog,
      I am not allowed to look back

at the earthenware that I floated away
   with your remains — your bone-ash
and unsinged Ganesh-shaped umbilical
   cord that bound you to your mother,
that bound you to my mother, and me.

Orange-yellow strings
   that secured the red-cloth tight
over the neck of this small clay-dish
   containing an ephemeral mix —
your fresh-burnt skin, tissue and bone —

   tugged at my heart relentlessly,
pulling me towards you,
   taking me back to a few hours ago
when at Lodi Crematorium
   I embalmed your recently dead body

with layer upon layer of fragrant Jharna *ghee*,
   touching your skin from the top
of your cold scalp to your brittle toe-tips.
   Both my hands were soaked in grief
as I caressed my open-palms over you —

intimately and somewhat unnerved —
with love, awe and pain —
    the dutiful hands of an eldest son
like a conductor's wand
    signalling a coda, marking closure.

As we rode in the ambulance
to the crematorium grounds,
    I remember my hands full of *khoi* —
puffed rice-flakes — releasing slowly
    from my clenched fists.

Flake after flake carried by the heavy air
    marked your life, its story and journey —
every road and path enroute,
    white-flecked —
the final map imprinted on black tarmac.

With half-trembling hands,
I put precious *navratan* gemstones
    in your gaping unbreathing mouth,
chandan-paste on your forehead,
    a pair of *tulsi* leaves on your shut eyelids,

marigold, jasmine, and *attar* scent
    the body over — the same body
that I'd recently clothed and draped
    with a crisp cotton sky-blue kurta
bought for you in Shimla.

I wrapped you too in the fine weave
of an unworn white-bordered *dhoti*
    brought from Santiniketan —
your gauze-bandaged mummified body —
    white, white, white, and more white.

Now only your ashes lie —
and my memories live.
    In the slow night's thick breeze
grey ash-curls slowly break,
    disintegrate, wither, float away —
dust, bone-white, nothing — *tabula rasa*.

MA | MOTHER
[Ratna Sen 18.12.1940 - 27.01.2013]
for Baba

As if in a dream, you disappeared
   unnanounced — untimely and unprepared.

The handwritten diary you left behind
   weepingly revealed your sordid, searing pain.

Grief-struck, I run around city's municipal offices
   rummaging through bureaucratic files,

seeking your death certificate for validation —
   as if losing you, wasn't loss enough.

ॐ

MOTHER
   haiku for Anna, Elizabeth & Peter

   our mothers' lives —
connected by a mere year
   of their own passing —

13.
GAAYIKA'R CHITHI:
NOTES FROM A SINGER'S SCORESHEET

Ami aakashe patiya kaan,
  Sunechi, sunechi tomari gaan,
Ami tomare shoonpeeechi praan,
  O go bideshini! ...
— RABINDRANATH TAGORE,
  'Ami Chini Go Chini Tomare'

Though we're apart,
You're part of me still.
— FATS DOMINO, 'Blueberry Hill'

BIDESHINI, BANALATA

I dream of pink and cream *dhakai* colours,
   of crisp-starched sari and honey-inflected throat —
a voice modulating *tulsi*, cloves and warm water
   to keep Rabindra Sangeet scales pitch-perfect.

I dream of Dhaka and longing, longing for
   that umbilical connect with my father's soil
and my child's early childhood — of Banani,
   Sonargaon, Faridpur; of Boi Mela, Chobi Mela;

of the long afternoons months-on-end at
   Samshur Rahman's book-filled Shyamoli room —
his wild silver hair and mischievous smile
   guiding my hands as I translated his poetry

from Bangla to English — syllable by syllable,
   word by word, phrases strung together to make
music in a new tongue. But tonight, I mostly
   dream of music — how its hidden heart-strings

bind and grace a friendship. "We are blessed —
   Allah-ki-duaey hain" — I tell my friend —
wet-lips, saliva, empty railway platforms,
   endless hot cups of tea, stories, dreams —

recipe for poetry, music and song.
   We are lucky to be graced with muse's magic,
lucky to fuel a spontaneous combustion.
   I dream of Bideshini with fresh white *champa*

petals pinned askance on her night-black hair,
   her pupils reflecting the well-worn *Gitabitan* —
its Bangla fonts and typefaces — lyrics imprinted
   like invisible tattoos on her salt wheat-skin.

Though we're apart, you're part of me still —
   I remember you Banalata, my Bideshini.
This winter night in Delhi is crisp as a song
   and sheer — as glass is — when dreaming.

JESSORE

I have lived in a golden cage — caged and tamed.
            I am mostly lost.

When I dive headlong
into the bracing winter winds —
        chill greets my face —
it is electric.

In my village,
I remember diving into the old cold pond
       blanketed by a layer of thick moss —
my naked skin, comforted by sheer green velvet.

🐦

DELHI

After a long concert, and after dinner,
I find myself unexpectedly with you
          in my room.

In this new space
      finding oneself is wonderful.

I was here and not here at the same time.

Later, I felt as if I had entered a story
        of an old familiar novel,
  a character I knew
     but had not met in flesh
  until now —
you, me, and my winter's dream.

🐦

DHAKA

Today's wintry morning sun
                is like frosted glass.

I am happy,
          cocooned in my embryo.

Nothing has happened —
          no, everything has happened —
                            no —

yet I am getting carried away
              by the toasted air
of this new season.

                    My heartstrings conduct
the tenor and pitch
      of a song
              I no longer have control of.

Light as air,
        the inflected phrases
waft in my imagined new home
                  with you —

alone, together, and all alone —
smiling, kissing,
              kissing, and kissing —
                    you are my song.

৩

NOWADAYS

all seems bright
    and energetic to me —

as if the winter fog
    has cleared it way

for sharp sunlit bracing
    days and nights.

Everything is lucid
   and crystalline —

colours over-saturated,
   weather perfect,

my hidden smile
   unhidden.

I laugh openly, loudly,
   and so much more.

I sing open-throated
   in sheer abandon.

My dreams are
   kaleidoscopic, vivid,

and my words now
   always gentle.

I have escaped from
   my old gold cage

just for a while,
   but it feels

like a lifetime —
   and it is a gift

I am grateful for.
   So I sing — and sing.

WINTER EVENING

Through the thicket
   and thickset clumps

of tropical groves —
   of mango, banana,

coconut and jackfruit —
   the winter evening

sun pierces
  its molten gold rays.

Streaks of sunlight
  try to illuminate

a *mis-en-scene*
  that goes unnoticed

to an everyday eye.
  This light's

tempered heat —
  not too hot,

not too cold —
  caresses my skin,

its minute subtle
  calibrations

played out with care.
  The amber light

bathes my body,
  casts variable shadows

on my white couch —
  the patterns

changing
  every millisecond

as the sun starts to dip.
  Right now,

the white cushions
  are dappled

and patterned
  by furtively left

gold-red lipstick
  marks.

Soon it will be dark
  and these shadows

on the love-seat
  will disappear.

But the lovers will carry
  in their mind's heart —

designs created
  by heat and light —

poised just the way
  the two people

wish it to be —
  soft-frozen in time.

🌱

REMEMBRANCE

Red sheds her skin
  to reveal pink tonight —

the dawn-pink reflected
  on the building

wall's canvas
  opposite my room.

Colours blush
  mimicking my heart —

their new song
  altering lyrics to melt

madness to sanity,
  sense to sensibility.

Burkha's hidden stories
  are now unveiled —

imprinted beautifully
  on your sari's raw red.

🦌

QUESTION

Your body scent
  and strands of long

night-kissed hair
  left on my pillow —

broken blouse-buttons
  on my bed-sheet — ·

a disengaged
  lone eyelash

curved, left behind
  as a question mark —

What
  happened? —

Reflecting quicksand,
  mirrors of time —

my answers live
  in your punctuations.

🦌

SHIULI

Ek mutho shishir bheja
  shiuli pathalam ... — SR

Shiuli flowers, slow-warmed
  in your clenched fists,

drenched in morning dew
  greet me with the scent

of your soft palm, fingers,
  and heartstrings. I weave

these tiny flowers, petal by petal,
  threading their stamen

filament by filament,
  into a delicate garland —

inking a love song's score
  in handwritten script.

Unknown to me,
  you wear these florets

in your silk-raven hair, and
  around your slender wrists;

singing my new song —
  Tagore as your witness —

tonight, and every night.

🦌

1.
PARSING

*Every great philosophy is finally
a confession, an involuntary memoir.*
— FRIEDRICH NIETZSCHE

2 SELECTED EARLIER POEMS [1980—1997]

SINGLE MALT

The single malt
    explodes

from its husk,
    swirling

in the cranium
    of its own

shell,
    flooding

the mind
    with images

that alternately
    switch

shutter speed
    and lens,

distilling
    sight,

that whisks
    away

from the mundane,
    what is

absolute
    and essential,

and leaves out
    what is not.

FLYING HOME

I meticulously stitch time through the embroidered sky,
    through its unpredictable lumps and hollows. I

am going home once again from another
    home, escaping the weave of reality into another

one, one that gently reminds and stalls
    to confirm: my body is the step-son of my soul.

But what talk of soul and skin
    in this day and age, such ephemeral things

that cross-weave blood and breath
    into clotted zones of true escape.

What talk of flight time and flying
    when real flights of fancy are crying

to stay buoyant unpredictably in mid-air
    amid pain, peace, and belief: just like thin air

sketches, where another home is built
    in free space vacuum, as another patchwork quilt

is quietly wrapped around, gently, in memoriam.

A BLANK LETTER

An envelope arrives unannounced from overseas
   containing stark white sheets,

perfect in their presentation of absence.
   Only a bold logo on top

reveals its origin, but absolutely nothing else.
   I examine the sheets,

peer through their grains —
   heavy cotton-laid striations —

concealing text, *in white ink*, postmarked India.
   Even the watermark's translucence

makes the script's invisibility transparent.
   Buried among the involute contours, lie sheets

of sophisticated pulp, paper containing
   scattered metaphors — uncoded, unadorned,

untouched — virgin lines that spill, populate
   and circulate to keep alive its breathings.

Corpuscles of a very different kind —
   hieroglyphics, unsolved, but crystal-clear.

MERMAID PURSE

        Leathery sack,
transparent, sewn tenuously
  with gossamer strings

        at its ends, parts only slightly, as
it reveals soft shark-skin inside
  and the silver tinge

        of its outer scales, as
the floating womb
  cuts gentle arcs, preparing

        for a later life. As its back
faces the translucent aqua light of deep
  sea, green and blue merge with

        the brown of the larva — and
the egg's oval matches the ballet
  pirouettes of weightless polyps,

        the languid unsettling of sand,
and the slow careful
  re-settling of its

        grains. In this purse, grand
score-sheets fill themselves,
  cadences marking

        the wavelengths of high trills and
low grunts of a mis-named 'mermaid'
  and the 'real' fish,

        inflecting tones and
scales of an ancient reed: the gentle song
  of water, weed, and the sonar suite

        of the under-sea. Here, an infant
shark muscles himself —
  learning the rules of shifting

>   maritime trade — and
> the rules to rule
>   his kinsmen, his kindred, his king-
>
>   ship of the ocean depths — and
> the politics of shrewd waves
>   under-cuts fluid mechanics.

NOTE: 'Mermaid Purse' is the name given to little packets where shark eggs are stored in their early stages of maturation.

THE PHOTOGRAPH

for Susheila Nasta, whose story this is

1.

I cannot remember the feeling of numbed pain
   nor fathom the sharp unexpectedness
at finding the grey-grained photograph:
   my father staring from the picture-frame
hung in the inner-most room of a Bombay flat,
   a secret my English mother guarded
so closely and furtively for sixty years.

Rani, the Indian queen, my father's first wife,
   my own mother, half and whole, long effaced
from our present lives by Englishness
   and false pride. A fact hidden,
truth unfolding, just hours before
   I was to board a flight into the memory
and reality of flesh-and-blood India.

2.

I disguised myself, hiding the daughter
   from my own mother to present myself to her.
Rani at her late age did not recognise me,
   but knew in her heart who I was, the intimacy.
The thread that wrapped her sari to her body
   was also part of the same umbilical
that once linked me to her, and her to me.

Only then I realised the sheer cotton, its strength
   that warmed and kept love intact:
sacred, silent, unspoilt and unspilled.
   It's only then I could see the darkness of my blood
and the lightness of my skin fuse so easily —
   see my father's unceremonious burial
at an obscure graveyard in an English countryside.

3.

I walked around the Mughal monuments of burial
    and peace, quietly with my friend,
retracing my past in Delhi, along ancient alleys,
    silk-shops, looking for delayed newsprint
that printed only part of the story, a story about
    the Cathedral of St Mary's that unknowingly
joined our school lives then, and our lives now.

I realised the unaged pain of secrecy
    and the power of revelation and re-discovery
that spilled guts and locked emotions enact.
    I had only remains of recorded magnetic tapes,
exposed bromides, memory and friendship,
    but enough to reconstruct mythic bodies:
imagined, unimagined, buried, but alive.

FRAGMENTED FEATHERS AND
TRANSPARENT BONES

In the rowdy noise of an unknown cafe, you
        lose a bag with three books — three books you
treasured, bought at a familiar book-stall outside a concert hall,
where some new jazz continued improvising itself all
        night. All of a sudden, unannounced Carnatic strains
        are heard, M S Subalakshmi on stage
           sung in formal scales, tones unlike
the chords you are familiar with, heard at a dinner last night.

When you hold a *mirror to the sun,*
        you get blinded not by its light, but
by the heat that scorches the pupils
and chokes all speech, stammer-still.
        If you hold a mirror to an arc-light, you get
        blinded by its very core, the over-heated tungsten
           reflection that coils and recoils —
while other orbiting particles

swimming innocuously, refract, fracturing
        the white into colour, in darkness. Appearing
gradually, blossoming in this black, *the colour of
a loved person's eyes* sparkle, *dreaming of*
        Java, or some unmapped archipelago,
        searching *for blue and red and yellow*
           fish. As the *city dies,* the night deepens, the
fusion fades, and the rhythm of the classical and the

blues slowly plays itself out — the concert
        finally ends — the people long departed, doors shut.
But in this empty hall — the stage
curtains still remain drawn, stretched
        out to the wings, as does the shaft of a lone spotlight,
        that too remains lit, switched on — perhaps an oversight
           of the overseer. But in this light
appears another sight,

an unusual theatre — a large super-imposed image
    of a bird — many birds — covering the entire stage,
their stories softly unfolding in a flight of metaphors —
fragmented feathers,
    beaks, and bones —
        transparent skeleton, hollow fossil forms
            finely sketched, etched permanently,
written with quiet wisdom, in ancient Persian calligraphy.

༃

RHYME ROYAL FOR AN UNKNOWN CHINESE WINE
for Vikram Seth

The furious bubbles spewing off my long-stemmed
    glass's brim, cracked, as globules of fire water
bottled deep green, scribbled in characters thick, steamed

    in insidious mint. This eruption of Chinese vapour
    couldn't restrain even the peaceful Yellow River

from a drunken meander, the Yangtze Kiang this time
tempting The Great Wall to sway, parched tipsy in this wine.

OLD ROOM

In my old room, I sit amid things
    that bind me to my past,
perfect in their sense of organisation,
    imperfect in their belief —
an old rusted spring,
    a pen's ink-crusted nib,
torn photographs, frayed memories,
    misplaced letters —
all re-sealed in my mind, a montage
    of re-photographed images and space
that alters and unalters alternately.
    But old rooms are like new rooms,
empty and full,
    depending on how you fill spaces.
Emptiness only defines
    the density of crowdedness.

    Suddenly, the furniture
alter their position
    to make way for a new geometry,
walls repaint themselves
    to provide a new canvas.
Spotless white sheets of seamless paint
    bury history that waits
only for a biographer's scalpel, a probe
    that may flake off the new skin,
but then, may not.
    I see old books now rearranged,
marked pages unmark themselves,
    tightly wrought phrases uncoil,
as old texts come alive,
    not new, not old,
but aged, undead, and memorised.

2.
SEXLESS LIKE ALPHABETS

They are men on the run,
Fuelled by bourbon and fear
Of things slipping away from them.
— ALAN ROSS, 'WALL STREET'
Death Valley & Other Poems in America

Generations of young people have come to New York to live —
earnest, glamorous, and passionate, full of sex and articulate suffering.
— ADAM KIRSCH ON RACHEL WETZSTEON'S *Sakura Park*

NEW YORK TIMES

Every morning
I scurry through the streets of New York, turn around the
        avenue, past the red and white awning of the Jewish deli,
   walk out with a bagel or croissant or spilled coffee,
disappearing underground, speeding

in a subway of mute faces, barely eaten the bite,
barely unfolded *The Times*, barely awake. Before
        I realise it's lunch-time, then
   late evening, being herded home with the flow
of humankind,

up and down elevators, escalators, staircases, and
ramps. I am back on the streets again, late night,
        though early enough to glance
   at next morning's paper. In this city, I
count the passage of time only by weekends

linked by five-day flashes I don't
even remember. In this city where walking means
        running, driving means speeding, there seem to exist
   many days in one, an ironic and oblique
efficiency. But somewhere, somehow, time takes its toll —

overburdened, overutilised —
as the tunnels seeping under the river's belly slowly cave
        in, the girders lose their tension like old dentures,
   and the underground rattles with the passing of every train.
After all, how long can one stretch time?

Illusions can lengthen, credit ratings strengthen,
even Manhattan elongates with every land-fill,
        but not time, it takes its own sweet time —
   the way it always has and always will —
not a second more, not a second less.

RAIN ON HOT CONCRETE

After the sweltering heat of the day,
    the evening fumed in its humid afterglow

while the lissome jogger
    on the sidewalk, cantered,

as the rubber of the sole sprung
    at every contact with the tarmac,

while the laden sky donned
    a coat of grey,

adding weight to the unusual calm.
    The runner's five-mile stretch

seemed longer today, as a sheet of sweat
    glued her cotton tights to her body:

taut, tenuous, every curve and muscle, sculpted.
    Her skin glistened with exhaustion

and the spray of intermittent drizzle —
    as the moisture of the sky and the skin

met the cement of the concrete in a sizzle,
    smelling of stale steam.

SCATTERED PIECES OF A QUARREL

*We listen while a dustpan eats
the scattered pieces of a quarrel.*
— VERN RUTSALA

Every night, for many years now I hear voices next door
through the thin of the wall, every core

of the crackling scream, like an old
stylus needle on a scratched gramophone record,

stuck. Every night it happens, shriller and fiercer
every night. At midnight, the ritual starts over:

the first conversations barely audible,
then the decibel levels, a plateau of maimed muffles

before taking off sharply, into the crystal
air of coded cries, on a steep delirious climb until

breaking glass-ware scatter smithereens
as the soprano of anguish startles a bluebird in

the nest outside, on the terracotta ledge
of my alcove. Every morning when the sun's edge

clears the neighbour's roof, I sweep the apartment floor
trying to extricate rolls of dust from under the doors.

They somehow seem to huddle in fluffy balls
insulating the crevices between adjacent flats, the same wall

that simultaneously separates and shares, just like the array
of dust coils clinging together, in fear of being swept away.

SUN STREAKS ON TELEPHONE LINES

In Japanese she said it was *amae*,
though the translation provided only a weak

dependency. The telephone rang all night, the next day,
and on and on for a whole year, in

metaphoric exchanges as the pulse
matched the tones. Tones of a new language

defied the stasis of the existing ones.
Even the sun's power couldn't scorch the linkage,

its rays streaking into a Brooklyn apartment, to cast
its bleach, roasting the innards, and a human being.

The same sun in the evening spread over the vast
view: over blackened roof-tops and the rippled bay,

its light tinting the metallic verdure of the Statue
of Liberty, the geometric axes of lower Manhattan towers,

and the silver criss-cross of telephone lines. On cue,
the calls came through, regardless, from another

island, the lines humming: *"amae, amae, amae"*.
Amae it had to be, after all, telephones work only on the

dependency of their senders and receivers, or else
why would such lines exist. The

sun had long set over the East River peninsula,
but had left enough energy stored, in excess,

for the unfinished conversation to carry on with her,
undeterred, in glinting solar pulses.

NIGHT IN TIMES SQUARE

At two in the morning at Times Square, I
    see steam escaping from man-hole crevices
as its fumes screen the changing colours
    of the competing neon signs.
A homeless person totters across the street,
    stiff and cold, totally unstartled
by the frantic yellow cab that misses
    hitting him by a mere inch.
Late nighters like me, amblers, whores,
    all gesture in silence,
in a language unknown, understanding
    each other with an everyday skill —
as the chorus of car-horns drowns the murmur —
    their lights scintillating with the tiniest flicker
of the many-coloured cathode tubes
    illuminating the peculiar-normal night.
A tiny island country
    capsules a continent, just
as the typical night envelops the square.
    I start walking southward,
down one of the avenues, hear
    the subway underground, its rattles
fleeing the iron-grates on the streets.
    Through the silhouette of the buildings,
appears a patch of night sky, and part of
    the moon, pale orange, reflected faintly,
in the glass and steel canyon
    of downtown, in the city of dreams.

SEXLESS LIKE ALPHABETS
for Joseph Brodsky & Maria Sozzani

We are all sexless, like a line of
alphabet letters in a classroom.
— ANONYMOUS

From the first babbles of a newborn lisping
to the ashed annihilation of the last skeleton,

mnemonically, life proceeds, pulsing
letter by letter, word by word, passing the baton

beat after beat, through stuttered phrases to polished facility
of language, and finally to that silence of inevitability.

That incipient whiff in the powdered spring
air of sprinkled pollen seeds and sprung stamens, preparing

to be stung, sucked, siphoned, and sipped
by the venerable black bee that carries — the lessons of love —

spelled out, slowly, one after another, pencilled
and documented between leaves, lettered in clotted mauve.

That a man here and a woman there, mistake
the one for the other, stand listless, admiring, regardless of sex.

That all of us are huddled together in chronological acts —
classrooms of meaning, learned and unlearned facts,

facts that fiction fulfills and knowledge informs, existing
like alphabets, like flowers, like men and women.

We, distinguishable, unseparate, pure as womb, sexless living
entities, indivisible, unhindered, passionate, whole, and human.

INSIDE CLOSED EYES, EVEN THE STONES COME ALIVE

held motionless by the dead
— JON SILKIN, *Six Cemetery Poems, I*

Inside closed eyes, close the eyes again, even the stones come alive.
— WIM WENDERS, *Wings of Desire*

This grey tombstone bears a name, letters looping in serif tails,
a monogram, some dates, and something in parentheses, effaced.

The sun rises very early in this part of the country, cross-
lighting only the solitary visitor who braves the frost.

Every morning for years, a woman in a black stole,
solemn, pale, lights three candles and places a red flower on the tombstone

that sits squarely, cracked, moss-ridden, wedged by two rocks
amidst overgrown weeds, discarded wreaths, and a shrub of

thyme. With eyes closed, hands clasped, body wrapped in dark linen,
kneeling, she prays long, silently, alone, with no one else alive, except

for the monolithic crowd of stone slabs and epitaphs.
She whispers to the stone at the close of every ritual, and

the inscriptions on the rugged granite listen, while
the stone shifts at the end of her prayer, staring wide-eyed.

SULPHUR

1

At dawn on Riverside Drive, after the frost
clears the trees, bare twigs usually glisten

at their ends, and remnant water globules
soon disappear at the call of the sun.

But this morning, after the hoar unwrapped the bark,
I saw new blooms, tiny, delicate, arched:

green sulphur on match-heads
glowing at the very first hint of light.

2

At the same time, many longitudes east,
across ranges, deserts and canyons,

a forest fire raged at Yellowstone.
Some spent sulphur erupted at first strike

as all the trees in a unified forest
burned in a choral conflagration.

Next morning, when the mist cleared,
every piece of bark, every branch, every twig

stood petrified, charred in columns of ash.
There were no globules glowing at the ends

as all the moisture was completely soaked
by the parched platoons of dead cinder.

There was no way to control the fire
just as there is no way to control the rain.

People, even experts, said the cycle
had to continue to its end.

Ashes, they say, replenish the earth,
soil for a new birth. In the distance,

the pyre's sacred sulphurous spirals
looped, linking the earth and the sky.

New York & Yellowstone National Park

❃

BIRCH

We replenished the fire's core
with a bough of new wood.

The aged logs — now hot coals —
glowed lilac and orange, igniting,

coated in white birch frost.
Cinder — now wings of flaked ash —

waited just long enough
for the next up-draught of thermals

to rise, float, and then descend —
scattering carelessly on our damp linen.

The Great Boundary Waters
Minnesota, USA & Ontario, Canada, 1990

PENUMBRA

    The sun came back out
from behind the deep-folded rain clouds

    after many days of ruffled uncertain
light. It emerged robed in tethered linen,

    just the way I held the sky in my hand
like a piece of crumpled paper. Bands

    of deep blue didn't seem to interfere with
the whites, and the cotton patches which

    were so transient, moved at the slightest hint
of breeze. I released the paper from my fist,

    tried to iron out the creases, but
couldn't. The folds had created a new terrain, just

    as the clouds in the sky never
repeat the same pattern over, ever.

A TUMBLEWEED

Driving through the gentle rolling plains
    of North Dakota, we headed west

for Oregon and the Cascades. The
    air was clean and warm, the

land was drought-dry
    and the tall wayside

grass, brown and stiff with
    the season's heat, resisted the wind

like a stubborn scarecrow. The road,
    at a certain instant, sloped

up, somehow meeting the horizon
    faster than usual. I spotted a lone

tumbleweed on one side of
    the highway, bouncing on

its spindles, crossing over to the
    other side. Somehow the

weed's long life ended with this death-roll,
    a mere crossing of a well-paved road,

while we traversed across the whole
    continent, in time which accounted for

only a whiff of our existence.

North Dakota & Oregon, 1990

THE DANCING GROUND

The moment I saw the brilliant, proud morning
shine high up over the deserts of Santa Fe,
something stood still in my soul and ...
the old world gave way to the new.
— D H LAWRENCE

Amidst the monotony of the clay-brown adobe,
    the still sky shimmers clear turquoise,
while the air travels clean and the light dazzles
    in a shifting pattern of shadow

and illumination, across this monumental terrain.
    Here, an unusual theatre unfolds: Helios performs
each day, on "the dancing ground of the sun".
    The ancient sagebrush landscape

paints itself on the New Mexican plateau,
    high in the middle of the vast canvas of
a grain-swept desert, where the southwestern
    sun bakes the mud dwellings of the Anasazi —

ancestors of the Pueblos inhabited
    the underworld first, or so it is believed.
The deep struggled to get out
    onto the land and into the light

through the tiny *sipapu* — the earth's navel —
    in the sacred circular chamber — the *kiva*.
But that was then, thousands of years ago.
    This century, here, the light still refracts,

pure, just like the earlier times,
    texturing O'Keeffe and Dasburg's palette, and
embalming Lawrence's prose with an elemental
    wash of primitive serenity.

Aztec National Monument & Santa Fe, New Mexico, 1988

SCAPULA, SCULLS & TWISTED HORNS

Twilight of permanent green lingers,
deep aqua of the surging Pacific

meets lush slopes of the rain-forest.
At low tide — logs, dead trees —

lie eroded, scattered on sand
like smooth bones — scapula, skulls,

and twisted horns — the architecture
of wind and water. Fifty miles south,

at Quinault Indian Reservation,
lie vast tracts of battered trees

and hacked stumps, littered
among random rusted blades of saw

and spirals of burnt-out truck-tyres.
Even the incessant rain could not prevent

the wrath of the logger's teeth
that gnawed mercilessly at the wood,

sculpting, cutting a new landscape —
a wasteland of tethered trunks.

Olympic National Forest
Washington State, 1990

ANCIENT MARINER: AN UNFINISHED STORY

1.

Water was calm
as the frost-bitten leaf,

no ripples,
just a sheet

of mirrored glass.
From this transparence

shot out, like sparks,
bright jagged edges —

steep walls of white,
washed limestone cliffs —

their faces
reflecting the glint,

rebounding
sun's unfiltered light,

2.

The 'c' and 'j' strokes
of our polished paddles

disturbed the
water's surface.

Every time we angled
our blades, slicing

the water,
its smooth surface

resisted
the ripples

we created
with every swing.

3.

This slurping
whisper

echoed loudly,
much louder

than the actual
sound,

like several
schools of whales

breathing
heavily,

quenching
their sonar thirst.

4.

Here, everything
was pure—

the water,
the air,

the light,
the sound.

In this
Ancient Mariner's

landscape,
we had not

 spotted
a single human

 being
for weeks.

 Only echoes of
Coleridge

 were heard,
as we

 paddled on
cracking ice.

*The Great Boundary Waters
Minnesota, USA & Ontario,
Canada, 1990*

˞

BRIDAL VEIL FALLS

 Each water molecule traces
its individual descent over a thousand feet,
 a path constantly remapped
depending on the wind's mood or strength.

 As the fall lowers its skirt wider,
the mist-spray sways
 the curving rainbow with it, as if
seducing the froth and colour in its moist.

Yosemite National Park, 2001

VALLEY OF THE GODS
for Amitav Ghosh

1. TAMAS

We got out of the car,
walked to the edge of the cliff,
and suddenly, without any reason,
jumped off
a thousand feet in the air
with Icarus' wings.

2. RAJAS

There was no reason
   why it had to happen there.
There was no reason
   why we stood there
amidst the vast
   copper landscape
on the edge of the amber rock,
   as the striated granite
braved the carving winds
   chiselling its sides.
It dropped, with no warning at all,
   as we looked down
and across, slowly watching the
   mist-layered canyon light
fading in a fugue
   of violet, purple, and blue.
The moon had just risen
   behind us, as we stood
clutching our fists,
   holding on to the barbed fence
that might prevent a fall;
   but not ours,
we leapt, holding on to nothing else
   but each other.
We looked on, as the moonlight
   washed and bathed
the Valley of the Gods,
   as our heartbeats

pulsed and matched each other's.
    Nothing seemed real
except the presence of
    two human souls in the wind.

3. SATWA

It was a realisation of brotherhood,
    inscribed and familial,
        bonded centuries ago.

It was a realisation of death,
    a coda
        that never really closes

because it isn't meant to.
    As the shadow lines
        staked their claim,

reason belied irrationality,
    death, life
        and passion, living.

4.

That night we drove to Goosenecks,
lay on the stripped gravel
under the crisp Midwestern sky.
The old Colorado meandered dutifully,
gorging ox-bows and new layers.
Together, we watched
the moonlight create a silver swish,
another rippled crescent,
weaving a curious circle of reason.

Colorado, 1988

CUMULONIMBUS

The highway dipped in and out of an uneven platter,
matting the earth's surface in an asymmetric curve.

I drove for miles on this serpentine coaster,
carving tracks on the undulating landscape.

From a distance, formations of low evening clouds
seemed like mountains formed of chalk and soil.

As we seemed to near these ash-shapes,
they receded farther away,

flirting in an air of elusive shyness.
All that happened thereafter —

we drove over many more hills, real ones,
up and down, over and around,

but never reached those illusive heights,
as they disappeared with the gradual fall of light.

Montana, 1990

3.
BRIEF | CASE

*All one's inventions are true,
you can be sure of that.
Poetry is as exact a
science as geometry.*
— GUSTAVE FLAUBERT, *Letter to Louise Colet, August 14, 1853*

COLOUR BAR

    What appears, is not. Black
is not black.

    What appears easy and white
is not white.

    Even the colour brown
on some skins and the ground

    appears tentative. There are
no greys to speak of, or

    to be seen. Colour bar is
fuzzy like the screen's static.

❦

INDEPENDENT HOMELAND

Bophuthatswana appears pock-marked,
    engulfed by the South African terrain.
Transkei, Ciskei, and Lesotho too, are arced
    to suffer the same fate:
tongue-tied, colour-coded, land-locked.

❦

DURBAN

Couched in the warm lap of the sea, Durban
    stays nestled in the gentle undulations,
opening herself to the world only at the mouth
    of the bay, carved out
in the shape of a leaping dolphin,
    her tail pointing to the mountains
of the Drakensburg, only a few hours away.
    The city rises and falls as easily as the waves
never allowing one the same perspective.
    But here, one is sure of two things:
the perennial sunshine, and
    the separateness of the races that do not mix.

ROSARY OF WAVES

Sampling the soil of new South Africa,
   I too, like yourself, walked along this Durban beach,
from Sunkist to North, Anstey to Brighton, and to Treasure
   Sands, bare feet eventually bleeding like the weeping sea.
Perhaps this was the same spot
   where you sliced your heel open, *dark ichor*
which even *three dozens of Elastoplast* wouldn't heal.
   From 1969 to 1991, you wrestled with the word 'with'
which kept reappearing in print inspite of scoring it out
   by hand with the replaced 'will', *feeling a bit like Achilles.*
That afternoon on the porch at Kharwastan,
   where your one-hour visit from the Congella lab
extended effortlessly to four, we recounted the syllabics
   of science, the mathematics of music, those that bind
poetry and friendship. Let that familiar scene
   unfold again, let *the sea my winding sheet* billow
and wipe off the threnody of isolation,
   scripting a new rosary, a rosary of salted waves.
The sea feels cold, warm, cold, and warm again, but
   that's normal for mortals, like life's own breathing.

❦

FEATHERS OF SNOW

A newly gathered flock of sacred ibises
   sits patiently, long-legged, styled on bare branches
of a lone, half-submerged tree caught amongst weeds. But

from a distance, they look like a frozen image:
   scattered feathers of snow, generously dusted
on dry bark, resuscitating its skeleton.

Botanical Garden, Durban

97 6TH AVENUE, MAYFAIR

Under the strong shaft of the Johannesburg sun,
    you sit in the old chair of your study, stroking
your cat, tiding the unsaid loneliness with your fingers

    that know the beauty of rhythm, enacted variously
under arc-lights and the sunlight. In this historic
    sprawling, book-lined home, you re-script for me

the Hottentot tale, repaint *Apollo Cafe*
    in this indeterminate *season of violence*, some of which
appears quietly in your London diary columns —

    the vicissitudes of the state. Across hemispheres,
both North and East, I carry your thoughts,
    replay The Poet Speaks, hearing the gentle cadence

of your voice, your voice that reverberates
    even now, just as strongly as it did from behind
the posters at The Market Theatre, listing your cast.

    The scent of the violet plant you hung on the porch,
still spreads, the sure solidity of an unstated friend.
    I returned to England today, after half a year away,

first in South Africa and then in India, to your card
    and the SABC tape, to be reassured once again that
in *time of our darkness,* the *war child, born of man*

    can still be resurrected, perhaps with a small prayer,
a simple one invoking familiar things: the preserved
    ticket stubs of *Hottentot Venus,* the fragrance

of uncared for weeds, the hand-woven Oriyan fabric,
    your inscriptions on the title pages, and
the reiterated rhymes at University of Witwatersrand.

SOUTH AFRICAN WOODCUT

Live township theatre smeared in blood and soil has
  carved *more* in this delicate piece of wood than

what's played out in innumerable scripts, repeated
  for years. The hollows of these eyes stare, animated

and frigid. Through their chiselled pupils appears
  a sight, a vision that condenses years and years

of unequal struggle. Thick lips, now too mute to
  protest once again, giving in this time, to

trade. But this mask, masks much more: the glaze
  of the rural varnish and the herb-paint's

primal colours preserves the ritual, annointing the
  face, charting history's altered course. On the

new stage, this face has more power in its passivity,
  more emotion in its muted, saintly serenity.

DARGLE VALLEY, MIDLANDS MEANDER

I am blessed with soil that pays for itself, you said,
    the stream, the clay, the sky, and the clear light.
A broken boat lounges carelessly on the pond,

its bow and stern rocked by an accidental inhabitant,
    its face guided by a lopped-off paddle trunk, found
just as accidentally as the re-birthing soil itself.

In the deep heat of the furnace, fired and superheated,
    double and triple glazing transform terracotta
as the local clay moulds itself from soil to shape,

precious as turquoise, calming as the earth's brown.
    After the passion cools, dots and stars are painted,
grooves and niches engraved, to deceive and hide

secrets of the earth, the wares, and their life;
    and also for the light to be stored and frozen
for another century, to be re-lit, years later.

Here in this valley of unobstructed beauty —
    frugal and healthy — the folk and Mingei merge,
along with the pig, Ming, the dogs, cats, and geese.

The pottery — half blue, half brown —
    like a lover, half available, half unavailable,
marries art and life in the silence of love and lies,

as the muddy stream flows past the vegetable patch,
    noiselessly like the soughing fires in the kiln,
reassuring one's own presence, here, and in life.

DALI'S TWISTED HANDS

To unsheathe our love, I had to break your hymen
    in my mind with my own hands (no, borrowed hands),
chopping the insidious plasma with the blade's
    passion that frightened even Damocles' edge. I

now have before me, blood-stained pieces of my past
    that once seemed so real and believably clad,
but, really, were merely part of a myth, a myth
    to which the present's locked door and unclocked time

testify. I have had to unwillingly abort
    our child and many others that were due, and
all the promises and faith which you
    severed seasonally, until the last time

when your unfaith struck, stuck shamelessly
    out from between the pages of your diary — that
dreaded letter, and many more even later
    to someone you were once with, unfaithful and trite

all along. But this time in your own beautiful
    savage way, you penned two paragraphs
that sealed all, and unsealed a holocaust
    whose fury even I could never imagine alive.

Now from amidst the ravaged landscape
    of my past, like the melted hands
in the twisted unexplained terrain of Dali,
    one clock unsprung setting time for a new time.

No more fancy bouquets of rare flowers,
    not even the pheromone-packed pollen glands
will germinate dreams of ourselves again.
    I now only want simple flocks of hyacinths, wild

and untutored from this year's fallowed land,
    soil from here, and not from some distant land.
I shall nurture them with my own hands
    knowing at least that one can always rely

on their return, unfailingly and faithfully each
and every season. I will mould the clock that
once refused to fit, the one from Dali's oil, but quietly
ticked on tirelessly, for me for years, now all mine.

❧

APRIL'S AIR

April's air in
willow-leaves ... a butterfly
floats and balances
— BASHO

Cherry blossoms bloomed when the fore winds
came, and wilted with the fall of the season. In

the paddy fields, planters flung their seeds,
broadcasting with parabolic precision, knee-deep in

slushy alluvium. A wailing child under a straw hat withdrew
quietened to graze at her mother's breasts. April air blew,

bringing with it a sniff of burnt red lava.
Silently the grand master posed: Bodhisattva

bowed and shot forth his limbs, fighting
the air, slicing every layer, as he danced, springing

the final *kata*. In the emperor's court, the scribe
recorded time in *tanka* and *haiku* on paper made of mashed rice,

while the fumes from the *saki* cup, swirling
intricately, etched primary patterns on pale porcelain.

MUSEÉ D'ORSAY, PARIS

Once a bustling old French railway station,
   now turned frozen with no tracks
to run, alive with fixtures and creations
   of the past, of art and artefacts
that vie for framed appreciation.

The bold steel supports, arched
   and straight, disturb the soft lines
on the canvas that once glibly masked
   nobility — glistening in oil — now behind
glass so high that you can only pass

from far to see its history. One of the
   higher floors opens onto a terrace by-pass
where the winds from Seine bring gently, the
   wet, settled on encased pyramids of glass
of higher art, from the grand palace across the

city's Louvre. While all along, the long boats
   spotted on their sides with myriad lights,
ply — full of visitors gazing at the domes
   above us — disappear downstream. At night,
these moving lights beam the facade stones,

where shifting shadows travel with the tides.
   Moments later I too disappear quietly
underground, tracking the Metro that slides
   across on rails beneath the river, to see
whether or not Mona Lisa really smiled.

4.
THE ACHE OF THE ARCHIVIST

In due course, in order to expose
For nothing — an entire interrogation
Vertiginously staging stories.
— CHARLES BERNSTEIN, 'The Ache of the Archivist'

Every great philosophy is finally
a confession, an involuntary memoir.
— FRIEDRICH NIETZSCHE

REMEMBERING HIROSHIMA TONIGHT

It is full moon in August:
the origami garlands surrounding the park

glitter as the stars — plutonium-twinkle —
remember the fall-out of *that* sky.

Tonight everyone walks around the solemn arcades
where lovers were once supposed to be.

In the distance, the crown of Mount Fuji sits, clear
on the icy clouds, frozen in time with wisdom.

Suddenly the clouds detonate, and all the petals,
translucent, wet, coalesce: a blossoming mushroom,

peeling softly in a huge slow motion.
But that's only a dream.

Tonight, real flowers are blooming
in the ancient Japanese moonlight.

ONE MOONLIT DECEMBER NIGHT

you came knocking at my door,
   I took my time to open.
when I did,
   there was just a silk scarf,
frayed, half-stuck in the latch.

CONCEIT

whether it is
metaphysical conceit
   or
human conceit,
the oddity of image
remains.

DUCKS

after the night's erratic rain
   a small pool formed
some mushrooms sprouted

their reflection
   like miniature ducks
from a distance

the price of eggs
   had come down
but the rain was transitory

NEONIC COCKTAIL

A neon light loomed in the murky gloominess.
The bar was no bar. Against the bar-railings

outside on the pavement, a man leaned, as if
it were a cocktail counter. He struck a match, lit

a cigarette, and dropped the stick in a consumed
alcohol bottle. The bottle exploded and burst

into a spirited flame — glass pieces clinked
against the steel bars — frothy fizz and

defaced crystals decorated the neon fuselage.
The man, or perhaps his image,

held up the broken bottle-neck to his animate
and inanimate mates, as if for another toast.

It was a unique cocktail — cindered spray,
powdered silicate and mixed spirits.

ॐ

THE FALL-OUT

A pencil balanced precariously on the edge
    of a desk, fell gently, on the floor,
        spilling crystal graphite.
Ants gathered at this chemical fall-out,
    and for a moment got
completely camouflaged under them.

The sharpener sharpened the bluntness
    into a smooth apex again — shaved wood
        in spirals patterned the floor —
powdered lead, dead wood, and live ants.
    Within seconds however, life
spans were shorter by inches, by aeons.

THE MAN IN THE HUT

In the dark corner of his unlit hut
    a man and his family lay, sleeping.

He was not really asleep,
    in the darkness his eyes were wide open

like a corpse struck with wonder.
    Rats nibbled at the left-overs,

the flame had long gone out,
    the lantern was dry,

so were a lot of things —
    his skeletal body, his wife's desires,

the bottle containing the spirits,
    the thatched roof, and even the

land he spent months ploughing.
    Nestled in the roof crevice,

a few pigeons had laid some eggs.
    Their shuffle caused part of it to give way,

and with a rustle of dry leaves,
    one egg fell. It burst open,

a mutilated womb, lay asunder.
    The moonlight seized this moment

to pierce one of the roof cracks.
    A sharp band of light shot through

whitewashing the faint clay walls.
    In a trance, the man watched on.

The ray focussed itself
    on the burst yolk.

Eclipsed, it looked like
   a disfigured moon,

glistening tremulously.
   The whole scene, radiant,

was enacted like a ritual.
   A mythical light had come

to take away the soul
   after an aborted life.

Suddenly, the clouds appeared,
   they covered the moon,

and the ray disappeared.
   The hut unlit, it was dark again.

Now, he could fall asleep,
   in peace. All this

light was quite jarring,
   unreal and unnerving.

THE ASYLUM

1. INSIDE

once a lunatic in an asylum
grew sane.

he thought,
he recollected, he created.

they all said he owed it to the moon —
his sanity.

while the others danced
in delirious hysteria —

as an invocation to Cynthia,
their goddess —

performing a ritualistic overture.
he sat and observed quietly,

distant, he didn't participate.
he was an alien.

2. OUTSIDE

out of his old habitat now
beyond the precincts of the asylum,

he met strange new people,
the normal people,

the so-called civilized world
with all its sanity.

but these people told him —
being insane is much happier,

it's more pragmatic
to react like a dumb stone

rather than a thinking human.
sanity diffused in insanity

or the other way around,
even they didn't know.

in the asylum he was mad,
or at least he was called so.

outside too he was termed mad.
something within him felt that

he revered the wrong orb:
after all, it was only

a satellite, which reflected
and had nothing of its own.

WOMAN OF A THOUSAND FIRES

I am made of silence....
My words fall at my feet.
— CHICK STRAND, *Mujer De Mil Fuegos*

In the windy courtyard
where my house once stood,
I labour heavy stone slabs,
carrying them in circles.
I am falling, the moon is

pulling at me. As everything swirls,
I hear the crickets hum,
craving in dizzy notes, until
I drop a stone in the empty well,
and hollowness echoes and murmurs.

Swinging, savaging the chicken,
I peel every feather plume by plume.
I caress your breasts. You, coy, quiver
tenuously. The ritual bleeds, snapping
the umbilical cord amid wailing hounds,

while whispers whistle the barren reeds.
The broom sweeps the brown landscape
as time collects in black mirrors.
Adorned, you, mythic, a red flower
in your hair. The mask-dance chants.

And again, charged, moans breathe
as wind whispers through fiery reeds.
I hear the world go round, but
I'll wait till the gale passes,
as you wait for me, wearing black.

LEANING AGAINST THE LAMP-POST

(ONE DAY) LIGHTING-UP TIME: 6.38 PM

leaning against the lamp-post
beneath the street lamp
a haggard skeleton
his synovial fluid dry
cracked and crackled with time.

                illumination shows
                  a silhouette
                    within
                      the
                  lampshade

feathered chatterers
perch on a matrix
of twigs and electrical wires,
peck at the
claustrophobia of the argonised confinement.

night-time destitutes
breathe
p a r o x y s m s of heavy air.
moths
f l u t t e r
around
s p o t t i n g
their blemished wings

                sweeping
                  down
                    describing
                    an
                    unquestioned
              arc.

sun rises to a new dawn.
the misty rays
clear its base
for a new occupant.

the day sees
trade, business brawls,
love, deceit —
claiming the sacrarium beneath.

the i n t e r m i t t e n t
vacant respite
fills the child's fair play.
the lamp-post, now cricket stumps.
a square cut cork
speeding down the street lanes,
just enough space between the wickets
until they are bowled.

concretised post has no vacancy.

evening,
night again.
witness to the whore's swaying breasts,
            murderer's dubious strangle,
            beggar's intestinal attrition.
all diffused in the murky glow of the neon.

suddenly the filament
s n a p s
to a blackened darkness.
whispering shrieks,
clamorous silence.

🦗

(ANOTHER DAY) LIGHTING-UP TIME: 6.42 PM

it's dark.
fused bulbs.
electrical genius of a spurious industry
or
a catapult's bull's-eye hit.

🦗

(YET ANOTHER DAY) LIGHTING-UP TIME: 6.53 PM

the lights fade into brightness after
and darkness thereafter
into a hallowed halo.

the skeleton rib-cage
remains,
devoured

by scavengers.
but the palpitating heart
throbs silently.

❧

i n t e r l u d e s
　of
occupancy

leaning against the lamp-post

THE TIN CAN

a child kicked the tin can   along the road
a jarring cacophony   at every boot

                              a cat   somewhere
                              le — a — pt   from a parapet to another
                              but suddenly   froze
mid-way   and fell with a dead thud   on the road

                                                      w
                                                      e
                                                      l
the pigeons from the parapet-nest   f
e s c a p i n g   the cat-call

at another kick the tin can
                                        c
                                        h
                                        o
                                        s
                                        e

                                              t
                                              o

                                                    r
                                                    o
                                                    l
                                                    l
                                                              along on its own
until it   f
            e
            l
            l   into a drain silently
                                        where the cat with a devoured pigeon
lay s w o o n e d   canned
in   the tin can

5.
INDIA INK

Pink is the navy blue of India.
— DIANA VREELAND, *The New York Times,* March 28, 1962

From the red to the green all the yellow dies
— GUILLAUME APOLLINAIRE, 'The Window'

KALI IN [DOUBLE] OTTAVA RIMA

Kali's curvaceous long lecherous tongue woos
    Shiva as it hangs loose, while she
tramples Him, stamping her beloved's breast, who
    lies passive under her feet, breathing still, as he
watches her wild swinging, with her own devil Ashoor
    draped around her neck. As she frees
herself slowly, crusade-ridden, victorious,
    bedecked, dripping thick in blood, luxurious,

she wallows in a crimson fashion,
    electric, juggling in hysteria the many-beaded
half-alive heads that adorn her aquamarine bosom.
    Resting arms, she wipes her triple-eyed brow, tinted
blue, her body prepares to make love, passion
    gliding as she dances on Shiva, the *Mahakaal* emptied
of infinite Time, while she guards her Time's own womb.
    Kali's rufous tongue woos Him, as it hangs loose.

॥

LORD JAGANNATH

The face of Jagannath lies tilted, coiled
    in anguish, its body contorted

        and crouched
foetus-like in agony.

The stroke
    that etched the jaw's gentle oval,

        disappears,
unannounced in a spiral swish:

A line one moment, a ring another,
    complete and incomplete,

        the end unknown, the sacred
sight known, remembered and revered.

The line, however long, never ends;
    Jagannath, however sad, never weeps.

DURGA PUJA

today / man will triumph over gods
— TABISH KHAIR, 'My India Diary IV'

1

Through the swirling fumes of the scented incense, the *arati* echoes
as the priest hums, and the *Chandipaat* chants in a scriptural rhyme.

From the bamboo pedestal she stares through her painted pupils,
the three-eyed *pratima* of the Goddess Durga —

resplendent, statuesque, armed with ten hands, on her roaring chariot,
her glazed clay demeanour, poised, even after the mythic bloody war.

Every year after the monsoons diminish, she comes, high from
her Himalayan palace — sculpted in fresh snow and open sky —

to the earth where she once belonged, her home with
her parents and people, reminiscing the quadrangle of her playful days.

Today, and for the next four days, we worship and rejoice
at her presence and her victory over Ashoor — the demon —

half-emerging from the deceptive black buffalo, as she spears
his green body crimson in a cathartic end to the Crusades.

These five days are hers, exclusively hers, even her children —
Saraswati, Lakshmi, Ganesh, and Kartik — fade in her presence.

For five days we sing and dance, laugh and cheer,
untutored, unlike the rest of the year.

2

The *dashami* comes even before we realise the *barone* is over.
After the mid-afternoon rites, the procession begins —

Durga's face totally effaced, red and white with *sindoor* and *sandesh*,
or perhaps it is the residual stains of the fervent worship —

her body weary, her coat of arms mutilated, often dismembered,
as she sits on open lorries, while the young men and women

dance the continuous drum beats, possessed — and Durga, now one of
the multitude, a rare frozen moment when the gods look human.

Though it may seem today that men will triumph over the goddess,
that her immersion at the *ghats* with mortal hands is real,

it is, like some myths, only an illusion of victory and sadness,
as she mingles, melting with the great silting Ganga,

her soft clay body browning the greenish-blue *bhaashaan* waters,
as we hear the receding din of the last offerings,

see the muted wick's faint glimmer on the floating earthen lamps,
and the moonlight's occasional flicker on the damp strewn petals,

as she wades her way upstream — miraculously through the
debris, dirt, sewage and homage of many unknown towns and villages —

back, to the pristine snow-crowned peaks, where Shiva
welcomes her home in an unusual dance of life;

while we, on earth, await her return the following year,
perhaps to celebrate, perhaps to pray, perhaps to forget

the life around, but perhaps to believe that *really*
the life force still lives, that the celestial cycles still exist

just as Durga visits, once every year,
just as, at the close of every season, she whispers from the heavens —

"Akhone aami aashi" — that I'll return once again — *Shashti, Shaptami,
Ashtami, Nobami, Dashami ... Shashti, Shaptami, Ashtami, Nobami, Dashami.*

A PILGRIMAGE TO MATHURA

Amid stone-slabbed lanes,
pigeon-hole shops,
rickshaws, bullock-carts,
people, and dirt,
walked a stranger.

Peras, Revris, Jalebis,
and all the local savouries lay uncovered,
open to devouring flies and humans.
One paid the price, the other didn't have to.
One carried the virus, the other got injected.

The stranger walked on
into an old temple,
with outside walls mossy and mud-ridden,
but for the shining dome that sat
time worn, tapering in a golden spire.

Inside, the air smoked and snuffed
in burning incense, saffron and fresh petals,
permeating the inlays on filigreed walls,
slated marble, and red sandstone, gilding
the glazed idols of gods and goddesses.

Amid chants, cymbals, song, and frenzy,
he saw devotion bartered, faith disrobed.
He didn't offer anything, just
a few words as prayer — a thanksgiving.
The priests, swathed in silk and silver,

sapped every pulse of emotion from the devout.
The worship carried on, just
as it had for hundreds of years.
One paid the price, the other didn't have to.
One carried the virus, the other got injected.

There was a river, and holy one too.
The Jamuna, with all its celestial allusions,
watered and gorged the earth, flowed on.
Old, maybe older than the city,
it washed Pilate's hands of everything.

A bird, one of the migratory species
came here for a new season.
But the stranger and the bird
soon left the city to find the truth,
while millions came here to find the same.

𑁍

GOVIND DEV TEMPLE, VRINDAVAN

Pink-buttocked monkeys leap from one lichen-layered eave
    to another, as the parrots' plumage splashes the deep red
of the wall green in patches: resident bees drone
    from the hives stuck to the ceiling, and the screeching
bats echo, flying in and around, tracing arced orbits.

Govind Dev stands steadfastly, propped with monumental
    blocks of red and ochre sandstone, where solidity and finery
of architectural execution are married in an art,
    both Islamic and Hindu, high on the hill in the centre of
Vrindavan, rising above everything around.

In 1590 when Emperor Akbar's general Man Singh
    supervised its creation, his cavalry bowed as they marched
past this splendour on the hill enroute from Delhi to Agra.
    Now, the surrounding tenements invade, inching their way into
every square of the courtyard space, and the pilgrims' walk.

Here, under the old sanctum, Krishna's idol was found,
    celebrated, worshipped, *rasa-lilas* sung by Chaitanya,
his followers, and people. Through four hundred years
    generations of devotees, bats, parrots, and monkeys
have lived here, prayed here, and changed hands,

but one fact has remained constant:
    Every year, on nights when the moon appears full,
its incipient rays streak through
    the main archway, lighting Krishna's forehead faint blue,
and the empty temple halls echo — *Radhey, Radhey.*

THE BOX-OFFICE HIT

The familiar score rings, lilting
   as the wide-screen extravaganza unfolds,
predictably, for three long hours,

   from catharsis to chaos, and
to that happy end, yet again,
   determined even before it begins.

The sweeping Technicolour splash
   dissolves, spliced in one big formula:
the Hindi film of Bollywood.

   It never fails, as the box-office swells,
the lines of masses meander
   out of sight for this seven-rupee show.

Maina Lajnu, or is it *Laila Majnu?*
   It doesn't matter either way,
a modern re-make, anyway.

   I stand, waiting, in the unending queue
for hours under the scorching sun,
   sweltering, sweating profusely,

with the hope of securing a ticket
   (which I may not even get),
and the air-conditioned retreat.

   I overhear a man behind me,
a factory worker of sorts,
   telling his friend that

he has seen the film ten times.
   Still he stands here every other day,
with a different companion every time,

   with the view to find something new,
or maybe nothing at all.
   As I inch along with this unregimented

swarm, the same man nudges me and says:
   "Bahoot baria philum, ek dum dream-like,"
nothing like his own life,

this seven-buck fantasy flight,
he explains. This evening, late,
   after the show is over, he trudges home,

again next morning to the factory-groans,
   every line memorized, even in his dreams,
just as in the film, as usual.

🦌

CALCUTTA | KOLKATA

The electric jewels of the night glitter
   steadfastly under the constant crescent
of the moon. Within one glitter, a coiled
   tungsten burns, in another, neon,
while the others reflected over
   the water's ripples illuminate quietly

the various colours of the dark.
   Some stars move, rotating as they go by,
others are left to fate to be fulfilled.
   As the blackness of the sky's blanket
deepens its colour, some fall asleep,
   others ponder, and a few like me never sleep.

The sun rises next day to a new morning,
   bright orange between the outlines of
the two familiar buildings across the Maidan.
   Last night's haze and this morning's mist
coalesce, as pigeons begin a new flight.
   Walkers trot, skaters roll, children play,

and from somewhere, an old dhoti-clad man
   carrying the night's wisdom, walks swiftly
across the open green with an umbrella secure
   under his weedy arms. The new sun colours
this day with yet another shade of pink.
   The marble of Victoria Memorial never

appears white in this light, just as the night's
   debris appear altered in the morning's blear.
The sun, its light, the people, their thoughts,
   colour the canvas,
their hues melting and moulting with
   the brush-strokes of every shooting glitter.

AUGUST 9, 1964
for Ma & Baba

Her placenta burned, turning lava-florid,
her womb stretching to its very last limit,

blue veins crying, full and wet,
   waiting for life — yet

another life, rearing to make an exit.
   A new entry — its

   sex unknown, until gloved
hands pull and reveal unformed

   flesh, wobbling around soft small
bones, out-weighed by an odd pear-shaped skull,

drooping, still connected to
   the umbilical, linked to

the very last. Now cut free from her breathing
   that only recently resuscitated his

   own tiny heart, he cries out loud to test
the validity of life itself —

   that squared triad of
sanctity — of birth, of life, and of

death — roaring,
   permanently stamping

his solar nomenclature — a leo-
   nine of a nine-day old

   month. A final tribute to her
labour, nine months of shelter,

her live chamber cloistering his helplessness,
   sharing her blood, breed, and breath.

VILLANELLE VARIATION FOR SHIVA

The *purnima* eclipsed, as the black tides turned,
unveiling moon's first flush — while violet skies parted,
creating a new form in red rapturous thunder.

Shiva, in a great wig of ancient hair, stalked
the ice-edged Himalayan peaks while he planted
his wrought-iron trident, the *trishul*. It's metal turned

electric, the cold heat scathing the shiny snowcapped
terrain. The old moon's rays over centuries slow-melted
the glacier — and from Gangotri's fountainhead thunder

the freezing waters of the Ganga flowed and eroded
the great northern plains that meticulously meandered —
carving the alluvial earth as it agelessly turned.

In the mountains, the same moon sparked
the trident points, reflecting the three-patterned
trishul, lighting the holy stream with a roar of thunder.

Nearby, the devotees knee-deep in water, prayed
to the triad-godhead watching the moon-face defaced
on icy waves — as the river's rippling currents turned
the orb's edges deep blue — in a slow-simmering thunder.

SUN'S GOLDEN SANDS

From Neemrana's curved terrace window
   high on the fort's porch, I watched
the evening sun dip low,
   as its amber rays flushed
the Rajput walls and the face of the cold
   landscape pink, orange, and gold.

History weathered the granite bare,
now being restored in sections,
stone by stone, pieced with local care
the old crumblings of time.

Many of us were there, invited, (exclusive
   I was told), divided, allotted and slotted,
to spend a night and day, in freshly painted
   rooms — ancient, regal — arched with promised
poetry, wine, and sunshine. That evening there was
   incessant rain as many poems were read.

Women with flowing hair — unveiled,
and men in fine drapery — plumaged,
watched, nodded, and listened,
and some even fell, unpredictably.

A month later, on the terrace
   of a different house, this too being restored
and unfinished, I clinked a toast
   with a friend as we peered through the crystal
and mauve glow of Benedictine, examining
   the hidden glint of a 5th Century Gupta coin.

Also a month later, I brisked through
the newly mown lawns, circling
the Lodhi tomb, this one restored
to the very last grain of sand.

Their walls echoed another friend's voice
    adding a 'to' to my name in a warm lilt.
Other afternoons we soaked ourselves
    in poetry, politics, and polemics,
which only the primal colours
    of Jamini Roy's paintings could reveal.

Then followed many days
of understanding, healing, and faith,
removing partially the archeological debris,
to unearth and discover

the sparks of the golden sands
    that made the carved figurines
of the imperfect Gupta coin glow, and
    the ALL CAPS sheaves of manuscripts,
revealing beauty and affection
    that went beyond diplomacy that rhymed.

The desert and city sands were gilt-edged
not for any specific reason,
but just that, the quartzite of the crystals
and the sun, ordained it all to be so.

TRANSLATING POETRY

Your poem translated itself so many times:
    from the incipient thoughts that brewed
    in your mind, as your mother tongue fumed,
straining to come together, trying

to emerge from shapelessness
    to a semblance of shape. Re-piecing
    together the shattered mirror, remoulding
and reflecting light from unknown niches,

the poem switched tongue and its skin
as the oblique image stamped its imprint.

But the translation wasn't quite done:
    it was fed into a computer
    to be processed, polished further,
and parts re-written, then fed again. One

strange beast of an electronic transmission
    ate the poem again, the fodder waxed
    and its shape reshaped. Then out of my fax
at night, a sheet of glazed emission

emerged, words on an unsuspecting tray:
A real poem defies translation, in every way.

6.
VESUVIUS

Suddenly the clouds detonate, and all the petals,
translucent, wet, coalesce: a blossoming mushroom,
peeling softly in a huge slow motion.
— s.s., 'Remembering Hiroshima Tonight'

An unannounced eruption reveals lilac
through the cracking skin of a dormant volcano
— s.s., 'Rivers of Fire'

MOUNT VESUVIUS IN EIGHT FRAMES

PROLOGUE

Death has an invisible presence
    in the Vesuvian valley, even the corpses

bear an insidious resemblance, that belie
    shifting shadows in the subterranean alley.

Death has an invisible presence,
    so does life, in its incipience and its ends,

linked, like two inverted arches, bent
    to meet in a circle at their ends.

Strips of zinc, metal coated in wax,
    bathed in acid, are scratched.

Year's twelve seasons reduced to eight —
    the image slowly unfolds its fate

in the half-light, under transparent
    protection of paper, moist and permanent,

etching the once-flowing blood stream,
    now frozen as rich loam, ribbed lava reams.

1

But the story began long ago: Remember
    the young couple, together

starting their life, their dream home
    distilled from that embryo's yolk.

The sight chosen, the view determined —
    Mount Vesuvius — this centrepiece

to be framed by an arched window pane
    of the bedroom's intimacy, and space.

2

Their house started breathing, piecing
    itself at night — the slow cementing

of bricks, supports, and the arch.
    The building traced its curve, its arms

locking tension in place. The spade
    like a magical brush made

everything circulate, outlining
    the movements, the inhabiting

of specific spaces, and the furniture's
    place. In a grand overture

the wooden bed with curved ends
    was placed right beneath the rails

of the window, overseen by Vesuvius.
    "Lava God!'" they prayed, "Bless us,

our love, and our curse". The union of
    flesh, blood, smoke, and bones.

3

That evening unfolded naturally
    and quietly, as deceptively

as the view's receding perspective —
    one that drew them to the mountain peak —

to its air, the snow, its dust, and fire.
    Fire engulfed their bodies, their

fingers, burning nail-tips, furrowing
    lines of passion on each other's skins.

4

It was freezing. The flames, frozen
  like tense icicles — hard-edged,

brittle, tentative, chilled, eager.
  The night brought a strange winter.

That night there was black rain,
  Everywhere — nowhere to escape,

except amongst the synovial spaces
  of their intertwined limbs, as

their bodies remained locked in fear
  and in death, around each other.

A marriage made in heaven, and in hell
  buried unknowingly — skeletal

remains transfixed in the passion of
  the very first night, unaware of

the world's changed face
  and the undone terrain,

now completely re-done, different —
  calcified, stripped, eroded, irreverent —

the bright skies sheltering the ruins,
  the dark soil protecting the fossils.

Death has an invisible presence
  in the Vesuvian valley, even the corpses

bear an insidious resemblance, that belie
  shifting shadows in the subterranean alley.

5

Years later, two grave-diggers (or
    archaeologists, or conservationists, or

restorationists), stumbled, quite
    by chance, upon this ancient site,

searching for something else,
    following a geological trail —

a chameleon path of buried ash —
    remains of civilisation now washed.

❦

Work began: Digging into the skin
    of the earth, defacing the soil, its

texture gradually ground further,
    reducing the grains finer and deeper.

Then liquid was poured, funnelling
    the volcanic shaft, clearing

the debris of the past,
    to unearth the past.

6

Then, a violent tremor, the plates
    shifted, skies darkened, there was rain,

heavy rain — a rain of redemption, healing
    the lepered limbs, slowly washing

the bones to the last brittle and grain.
    Death has an invisible presence

in the Vesuvian valley, even corpses
    bear peculiar insidious resemblance.

7

Now, people come in great numbers, pay
    to see the same space —

the house, the room, that bed,
    the couple mummified as they last slept,

left unmoved, untouched, unaged.
    Mount Vesuvius still guard their gate

and the view — the outside
    of the past, and the life, inside.

8

The dead: All neatly packed
    in small square groups, and

in even multiples of eight,
    nailed, framed, and glass-encased.

Even the new gravediggers pay,
    the elderly mountain pays

too — in twos, fours, and eights.
    Pompeii remains, uncontained.

❦

Strips of zinc, metal coated in wax,
    bathed in acid, now re-scratched.

Year's twelve seasons reduced to eight —
    the image slowly unfolding its fate

in the half-light, under transparent
    protection of paper, moist and permanent,

etching the flowing blood stream, life
    frozen, yet unfrozen, rich lava, alive.

EPILOGUE

Death has an invisible presence
    in the Vesuvian valley, even the corpses

bear an insidious resemblance, that belie
    shifting shadows, in the subterranean alley.

Death has an invisible presence,
    so does life, in its incipience and its ends,

linked like two inverted arches, bent
    to meet in a circle at their ends.

[inspired, in part, by a series of etchings by Peter Standen]

*He who knows no foreign language
knows nothing of his mother tongue.*
— JOHANN WOLFGANG VON GOETHE

All translation is interpretation.
— DANIEL WEISSBORT

*To create a poem means to translate
from the mother tongue to another tongue...
No language is the mother tongue.*
— MARINA TSVETAYEVA
in a letter to Rainer Maria Rilke

3 SELECTED TRANSLATIONS [1997—2015]

JIBANANANDA DAS
Translated from Bengali

BANALATA SEN

For a thousand years I have walked this earth's passage
   by day and night — from Lanka's shores to Malay's vast seas.
I've travelled much — been a guest at Bimbhishar and at Ashok's courts,
   stayed in the distant nights, in the town of Bidharba.
I'm long worn-out; around me waters of sea and life have endlessly swirled.
   My only peace — a fleeting moment snatched with her —
      Natore's Banalata Sen.

Like the dense ink-night of Bidhisha, her hair — black, deep black;
   her face — like the delicate-weave of Shrabasti's filigree-frieze.
Just as a lost boatman, rudderless, tossing in the far seas
   chances upon a lush-green Isle of Spice,
I too caught a sight — saw her, a mere glimpse in the dark. Gently, raising
   her eyes like a bird's nest, she whispered: 'Where *were* you, all this while?'
      [And there she stands at my dream's end — my own Banalata Sen].

With soft-settling hiss of dew, evening closes the day's end;
   kites erase from their wings, sun-stain smell of flight.
When colours of the earth gently fade, fireflies light up their palette,
   and old songs find new lyric, old stories new score.
Birds return home, so do the rivers; as life's trade — its give-and-take — ceases.
   Only the dark stays. And just as it remains, so does
      sitting by my side, face to face, my own Banalata Sen.

RABINDRANATH TAGORE
Translated from Bengali

'IN SCHOOL, YAWNS'

In school, yawns
  Motilal Nandi —
    says, lesson doesn't progress
      in spite of concentration.
Finally one day on a horse-cart he goes —
tearing page by page, dispersing them in the Ganga.
      Word-compounds move
        float away like words-conjoined.
      To proceed further with lessons —
        these are his tactics.

३

'IN KANCHRAPARA'

In Kanchrapara
  there was a prince
[wrote but] no reply
  from the princess.
With all the stamp expenses
will you sell off your kingdom?
Angry, disgusted
  he shouted: "Dut-toor"
shoving the postman
  onto a bulldog's face.

'TWO EARS PIERCED'

Two ears pierced
   by crab's claws.
Groom says: "Move them slowly,
   the two ears."

Bride sees in the mirror —
   in Japan, in China —
thousands living
   in fisher-folks colony.
Nowhere has it happened — in the ears,
   such a big mishap.

'BIRD-SELLER SAYS, "THIS IS A BLACK-COLOURED CHANDA."'

Bird-seller says, "This is a black-coloured chanda."
   Panulal Haldar says, "I'm not blind —
It is definitely a crow — no God's name on his beak."
Bird-seller says, "Words haven't yet blossomed —
   So how can it utter 'father' 'uncle' in the invocation?"

NOTE: All four poems are taken from the Visva Bharati edition of Tagore's nonsense verse, *Khapcharra* (Out of Joint). They are all untitled, so I have used the first line of each poem as their symbolic title. 'In school, yawns' appears on page 4, 'In Kanchrapara' on page 5, 'Two ears pierced' on page 10, and, 'Bird-seller says, "This is a black-coloured chanda."' on page 11. These translations have appeared in *World Literature Today*, *Aria\Anika*, and *The Essential Tagore* (Harvard University Press & Visva Bharati).

MANDAKRANTA SEN
Translated from Bengali by the author & SS

A LETTER FROM LESBOS

Blood is on her face, chest; blood is in between her legs —
This wild smell of blood has made me crave and beg.

This fleshy smell of blood has made me lust for more —
In the sea of desire, *this* is the triangular shore.

Is she a man, or a woman? — Who's there to determine?
I've seen her in the dark — she is my light, she's mine.

MITHU SEN
Translated from Bengali

MAGPIE, SPARROW

In my home's many rooms — sparrows, magpies nest.
I weep on their wings — they too weep embracing me.
Eye's lashes embrace tears — tear's lashes embrace eyes.
In my home's many rooms — sparrows, magpies nest.

If sadness is bird's wings — if sadness is wind's flight,
real sadness is mourning. Is real sadness dying?
That death is ice-still eyes — eyes' tears enclosing ash.
In my heart-chamber's many rooms — sparrows, magpies nest.

SHAMSUR RAHMAN
Translated from Bengali with the poet

LOVE'S OVERTURE

I know who I desire — the one whose eyes blossom.
In a moment — happiness will spark like light.
I do not tremble in fear, nor sway in hesitation —
Now at night, I'll light a thousand lamps —
adorn your path hoping you would come.
If she walks here on the path where her heart's shadow falls —
blossoming like flowers — blossoming like stars —
[then, light will] burn all night, shine *all* night.
I know whom I desire, but I do not reveal her name
in a crowd without direction; only dream sounds
as my heart reveals her name, a delicate name.

AMINUR RAHMAN
Translated from Bengali

LOVE: 5

My heart's sky contains you, Nilima
A star beyond the galaxy
A lotus in the river
Emerging as a new woman.

FAZAL SHAHABUDDIN
Translated from Bengali

SPELLBOUND

Like an angry pyre, the wind leaps —
Fallen leaves scurry, fly around
like countless birds —
Skies strike up an impossible score —
Shadow's continuous restless-run
fills the earth.
And after that? —

Breeze, fallen leaves, overcast skies —
Shadow's continuous restless-run
everything —
Like a still-born wail of a cry —
In a moment, all vanishes from sight — existence
where sea ebbs and flows.

Till far away, one can see
land's concrete plains —
part of the earth seem ancient,
and a woman thirst-ridden.

KAIFI AZMI
Translated from Urdu

ONE KISS

The moment I kiss these beautiful eyes —
hundred candles in the darkness, glow-and-glitter.

What flowers, what buds, what moon, what stars —
all adversaries bow — at their feet — head lowered.

They begin their dance — the idols of Ajanta,
as the long close-lipped caves start to sing.

Flowers bloom in unkempt wilted gardens —
on thirst-wrenched earth, clouds collect-and-hover.

Momentarily, the world relinquishes crime —
momentarily, all stones start to smile.

❧

GULZAR
Translated from Urdu

SKETCH

Do you recall that day
when you sat at my table —
On a cigarette pack,
a small sapling's
sketch you had made —

Come here, see —
on that plant now, flowers appear!

ASH

Behind bars, even in the rebel's eyes
ash has begun to shed.
When coal-embers remain unfanned for long —
then even in the flames' eyes
pearl-white cataract start to appear!

SACHCHIDANANDA VATSYAYAN AGYEYA
Translated from Hindi

SUNSET

Sunlight —
a mother's laughter reflected on her child's body —
the rays spread, floating
over new pines crowning the hills beyond.

A song:
without heart's heavy aches,
without argument and acceptance,
says:
'No, one will *no* longer need to return again.'

🌿

ATAL BIHARI VAJPAYEE
Translated from Hindi

PAIN

The room, empty —
my pain, double

> The cricket's cry —
> severs my insides.

The shut sky —
choking my breath.

🌿

KAILASH VAJPEYI
Translated from Hindi

MAKE A WAY

Make a way
so that eye is not shut —
still, the world vanishes.

As drowning is inevitable —
do not trust the boat,
but always trust the river.

KUNWAR NARAIN
Translated from Hindi

QUESTION

Through stars' blind alleyways
echoes proud *laughter* ...
this is my question:
Immense, grotesque;
my piercing gaze's heat-intense probe —
a question that made the big snowman
melt ...
was that your answer?

ASHOK VAJPEYI
Translated from Hindi

PLAY

I spread out earth's green bed
I pull in sky's blue veil
I place sun and moon on two pillows
I remove grass's attire
I indulge in play with you.

SHAMSHER BAHADUR SINGH
Translated from Hindi

AN EMPTY LONELY PATH, A SAD WATERFALL

An empty lonely path, a sad waterfall.
On a fuzzy cloud-line rests the entire sky,
where that young dark girl
had once smiled.

SAVITA SINGH
Translated from Hindi

WOMAN IS TRUTH

All around, sleep —
thirst is everywhere —
in half-awake state,
in dream's wakefulness
where sea ebbs and flows.

Till far away, one can see
land's concrete plains —
part of the earth seem ancient,
and a woman thirst-ridden.

❧

RATI SAXENA
Translated from Hindi

FEAST TIME

Give me such a timetable
where my own time isn't there.

Then give me a timetable
where only my own time exists.

I will drink both timetables
like thick milky-mango-juice.

Then time will be inside me,
and I will be free of it.

❧

KEDARNATH SINGH
Translated from Hindi

SELF-PORTRAIT

One line
drawn across earth's latitudes,
where
　close to the sun's orbit,
　it loses itself —
　That is where
　　I stand.

Fisherman's
　net,
　pulled out from the river,
　lie
　　draped over my rough shoulders —
　　This is my town.

Smile's glimpse
　strung on suspended wires,
　buffeted by the breeze,
　hang low —
　　There
　　is my home.

　A small house,
　and this small abode
　contain many views.

Every view
　in haste
　　capture other views,
　　and where they touch —
　　There
　　　I live.

MANGALESH DABRAL
Translated from Hindi

TOUCH

Touch the things that are kept on the table in front of you
Clock pen-stand an old letter
Idol of Buddha Bertolt Brecht and Che Guevara's photos
Open the drawer and touch its old sadness
Touch a blank sheet of paper with the words' fingers
Touch like a pebble the still water of a van Gogh painting
Starting life's hullabaloo in it
Touch your forehead and hold it for a long while without feeling shame
To touch it isn't necessary for someone to sit close
From very far it is possible to touch even
Like a bird from a distance who keeps her eggs protected

'Please do not touch' or 'Touching is prohibited' don't believe in such phrases
These are long-running conspiracies
Religious-gurus holding flags wearing crowns and shawls
Bomb-throwers, war-raisers indulge in for keeping us apart
The more dirt the more waste they spit
Only by touch can they be cleansed
Touch you must even though it turns things topsy-turvy
Don't touch the way gods priests bigots devotees disciples
Touch each others' feet and heads
Rather touch the way the tall grass appears to caress the moon and stars
Go inward feel the moist spot touch
See if it still remains there or not in these ruthless times.

ANAMIKA
Translated from Hindi

SALT

Salt is earth's sorrow and its taste.
Earth's three-fourths is brackish water,
and men's heart a salt mountain.
Weak is salt's heart,
very quickly it melts,
it sinks in shame
when plates are flung
due to salt's varied strength.
There stands —
a government building —
like a salt shaker —
shakes with much sophistication, sprinkles
salt in my wound.
Women are the salt of the earth,
they have all the salt in the mould of their face.
Ask those women
how heavy it feels —
their saline faces?
All those determined to pay the salt's price,
all those who couldn't betray their masters
have annoyed the seven seas and
the revolutionaries.
Gandhi knew the salt's worth
as do the girl-guava-sellers.
Whether or not something
stays in the world,
there shall always be salt.
God's tears and man's sweat —
this is salt
that balances the earth.

MOON CHUNG HEE
Translated from Korean with the poet

WILLOW

He etched blue flowers
    on my arms —
Blue flowers
    that tied
my skin, my whole body,
    my spirit, and my life.

Just on one summer day,
    and after that —
Finally, when I go
    to my tomb —
I will forever clutch
    the blue flowers to me.

CAI TIANXIN
Translated from Chinese with the poet

BOSTON

Bridges — connecting two shores,
    watered by the bay.

Ocean — rising tides bring with it —
    shells and youth.

Sky — pure blue — a few clouds
    ripple with the breeze.

Times — I visited her —
    no more than just three.

Ocean — tides ebb, leaving behind
    pearls and truth.

Name — my name — two sighs —
    never a thought to stay, here.

AVRAHAM BEN YITSHAK
*Translated from Hebrew with Yehuda Amichai,
Daniel Weissbort, Stanley Moss & others*

THE LONELY SAY

Day after day the sun's light melts and moults
    As night yearns for darkness.
In the autumn's heap, gather continuing summers
    As the world sings in its lamentation.

    Tomorrow, stricken with the absence of words, we die;
And on that day, we shall stand at death's gate.
    As the heart celebrates the closeness to God,
It will do so, in joy and repentance, in fear of betrayal.

Everyday brings the sun's light,
    And every night the stars,
And upon the lips of some, the song stammers still.
    In seven ways, we part; but return only by one.

❦

AMIR OR
Translated from Hebrew with the poet

ARCHER

My skin is swifter than the wind,
my arrow is swifter than my legs,
I strip my clothes off,
[strip off] my words, my face —
on and on. High in the sky
the hawk diving in the breeze
is too slack for me.
On and on, my life,
beyond my life.
Between the pinnacle and the abyss
into the void, into the windless quiet,
I
leap
seize my arrow between my own teeth.

SHIRIN RAZAVIAN
Translated from Persian with the poet

IT IS WINTER

The ground is ice-cold
with many layers of frozen water,
unbreakable icicles
their facets cut like diamonds.

It is snowing —
my hands freeze
as my heart turns
blue, and more blue.

An old myth says
that everyone's a snowman —
and on them, I carve
smiles, determinedly — but

they lie through their teeth.
Their heart is too cold, white
like frozen earth.
It is August,
but the weather is sheer winter.

DITTE STEENSBALLE
Translated from Danish with the poet

THERE LIES

There lies
    years gone by

in the night-sleep dreams,
    like difficult children,

like animals — you.

ZORAN ANCHEVSKI
Translated from Macedonian with the poet

MY LITTLE ME

When I fenced in my little me
and said to myself *This is mine*
It grew,
became my dictator —
handsome and greedy.
Now I prepare for rebellions,
ambushes;
I plot evil,
I hire traitors, assassins.
But in fact
as the lowest of all serviles,
I grovel before its feet
and flatter, salivating at its throne.

PETKO DABESKI
*Translated from Macedonian
with Natasha Dabeski and the poet*

MOMENTS AND MOMENT

It is that time when every moment —
even with the naked eye —
I can see each leaf's growth
maturing on the tree,
making the gaps between the leaves
on the tree's crown subtly diminish.
It is in this moment, in a photograph,
I see a woman
of over a hundred
holding a hoe —
bent double, hunched groundwards —
digging.
It's at this very moment, my voice exclaims:
beauty, beauty!

EWA SONNENBERG
Translated from Polish with the poet

ON THE SHORE

What we cannot name
will become history

It may still come back
and become history

What can preserve touch
will become history

History which we haven't shaped —
she knows more than us
since she speaks herself

History only for forgiveness

🌿

VERONICA ARANDA
Translated from Spanish with the poet

XV

I always went by the inertia of furtive love,
that of the port cities: Buenos Aires
with its edge of suburbs, old Havana,
Lisbon, and mysterious Biralbos.
The bandoneón and the guitars —
their chords weaving red and black;
the theatres of penumbra,
open fabric in suitcases,
rooms with 20 years of nicotine,
and the simple bar where they all gather —
the silence of liquor, as sorrows disappear.

🌿

MATTEO CAMPAGNOLI
Translated from Italian with the poet

from **IN SPAIN** *[a version-in-progress]*

IV.

if this were a true poem
its lines would shine in the sun
like a blade-sliver of a brook
shining at the bottom of a gorge —
it would quiver in asphalt-heat
radiating Seville's siesta-hour,
when balconies shut
and every street leads to an end —
it would contain
all the sorrow echoing "Spain" —
and in a sudden truce of blue tiles
under a Granada patio —
you will hear accent of storks
alighting on Alcalá
in the surround quiet
of vowels, bell-towers, and
madness of black-wings rising
from Goya's dream —
as if they were true — but only
if this were a true poem

SERGIO CLAUDIO F. LIMA
Translated from Portuguese with Celia Cymbalista and the poet

THE BODY [OF A WOMAN] SIGNIFIES

A mulher e o corporal o mais elevado. — NOVALIS

Devemos comer de novo da arvorce do conhecimento, para retornarmos ao estado de inocencia. — HEINRICH VON KLEIST

Originality of imagery is not important — the collage of existing images has proved more fruitful than creating fresh images in evoking consciousness to transcend artificial boundaries of 'reality'. Hence Duchamp's statement that "art is not a creative activity, but a means to expand consciousness". — JOHN LYLE

I   The sight of love is definitive.
II The way of seeing is the way/an expression of being.
III The doing is the development of thinking, of thought.
IV The act of action circumscribes, and the sense opens the field of art.
V   The act of acting: "Only the one who knows this, the one who does not know, does not do." (— REX)
VI The sense is the tension (in tension), one which forms, broadening ...
VII ... the support of the initial thought.
VIII The sense is rhythm.
IX (The sense is relation).
X   The rhythm: It *has* to do with the feminine.
XI — the form of the body define the rhythm. Thus
XII starting from the loving, the amorous forms
XIII significance, a meaning of knowing and knowledge.
XIV For example: by walking she is giving a new imprint,
XV she makes a gesture, a drawing.
XVI She gives shape, creates an emblem [of my existence as a body].
XVII (note-se *andando* / that in the act walking: the trajectory is important, because
XVIII it is the unfolding that configures / a representation)
XIX The body [of a woman] signifies.
    THE BODY MEANS.

NOTE: This poem is a translation of the essential framework/content of the book, *O Corpo Significa* by Sergio Lima (Sao Paulo: Edart / Livraria Editora Ltda, 1976), which operates on a complex multi-tiered level comprising of 232 'A4-format' pages]

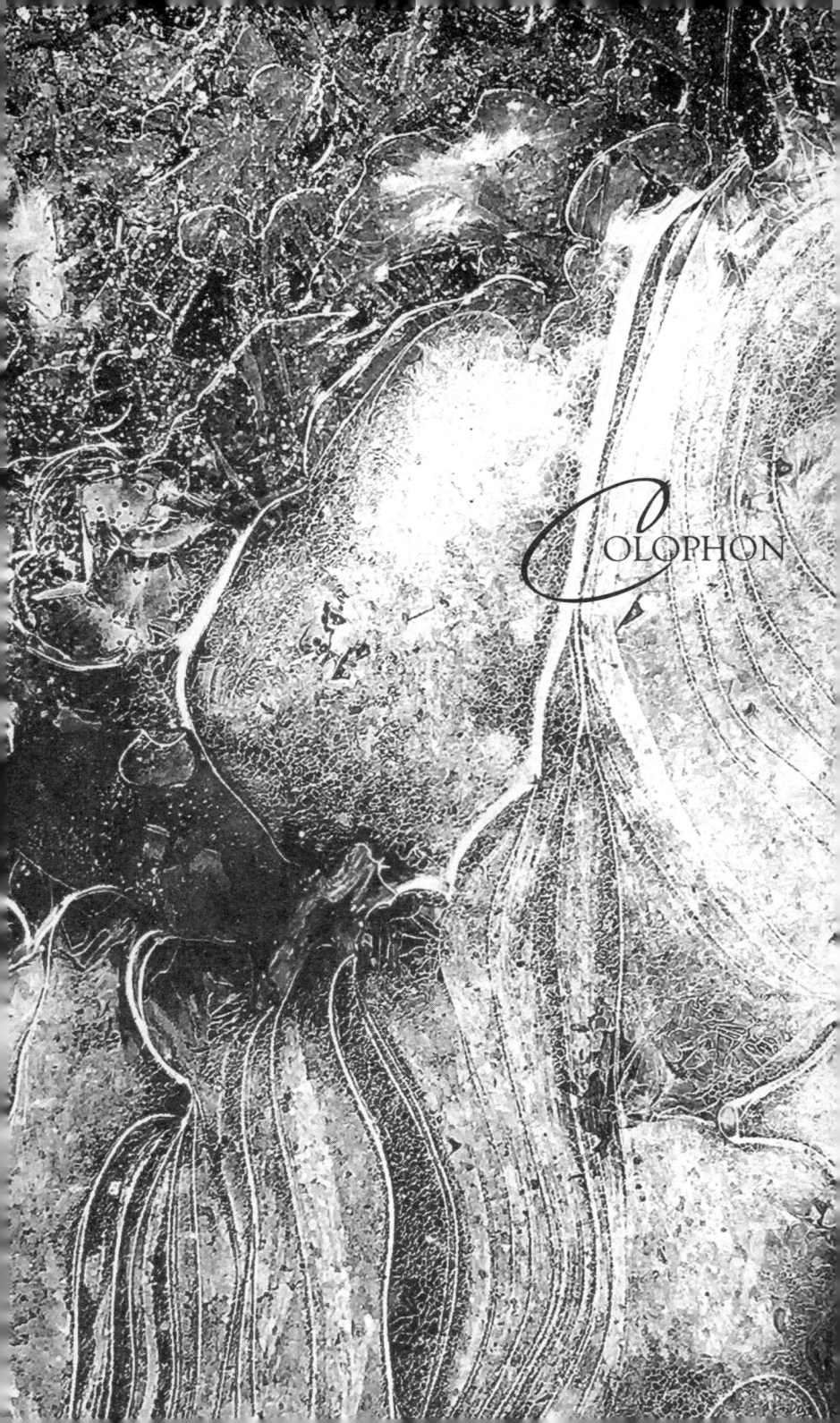

Colophon

AUTHOR NOTE

Certain readers who may be familiar with my older poems [in the various British, American, Indian & other editions that have appeared earlier], may wonder as to why there are minor changes in a few of them. To this, I can only reiterate the late Sir Stephen Spender's thoughts: "I can only say that I do not rewrite poems in the sense of adding new material. But — apart from those occasions when something seems so inept that it cries out to be improved — I sometimes remember, when I look at a poem, what I had originally meant to say: and I have another shot at saying it".

PUBLISHERS' NOTE

The publisher have made every effort to trace copyright holders, but in some cases without success. We shall be very glad to hear from anyone who has been inadvertently overlooked or incorrectly cited, and will make the necessary changes at the first opportunity.

ABOUT THE TYPE

The book's main text is set in Adobe Caslon Pro. William Caslon released his first typefaces in 1722. Caslon's types were based on seventeenth-century Dutch old style designs, which were then used extensively in England. Because of their remarkable practicality, Caslon's designs met with instant success. Caslon's types became popular throughout Europe and the American colonies; printer Benjamin Franklin hardly used any other typeface. The first printings of the American Declaration of Independence and the Constitution were set in Caslon. For her Caslon revival, designer Carol Twombly studied specimen pages printed by William Caslon between 1734 and 1770. The OpenType "Pro" version merges formerly separate fonts (expert, swash, small caps, etc.), and adds both central European language support and several additional ligatures. Ideally suited for text in sizes ranging from 6- to 14-point, Adobe Caslon Pro is the right choice for magazines, journals, book publishing, and corporate communications.

Arial has been used as the typeface for individual poem's titles. Its contemporary sans serif design contains more humanist characteristics than many of its predecessors and as such is more in tune with the mood of the last decades of the twentieth century. The overall treatment of curves is softer and fuller than in most industrial style sans serif faces. Terminal strokes are cut on the diagonal which helps to give the face a less mechanical appearance. Arial is an extremely versatile family of typefaces.

ACKNOWLEDGEMENTS

For a huge book like this that spans 35 years of professional writing life — to try to list and acknowledge every poem that was published in the varied and numerous media around the world would be a project-length challenge, very time-consuming, and perhaps a logistical nightmare. So let me take refuge in a general thank you to all the producers and editors of various publications worldwide, in which the bulk of the poems in this book, many in earlier versions and some under different titles, first appeared. However, some of the more recent acknowledgements I can remember, would include:

'Choice' in *The HarperCollins Book of English Poetry*, *The Literary Review*, *Yellow Nib*, and *Prairie Schooner* (Pushcart Prize nomination 2013); 'Gaza' and 'MH-17 Crash' in *The Hindu* and *The Daily Star*; "Gayika'ar Chithi' in *Bengal Lights*, *Six Seasons Review* and *Indian Literature*; 'Banyan' in *Initiate: Oxford New Writing* (Blackwell) and on Poetry Society UK Online (Poetry Society [UK] Stanza Joint Runners-Up Prize Winner 2012); 'A Blank Letter' in *Language for a New Century* (Norton) and *Postmarked India: New & Selected Poems* (HarperCollins); 'Desire' in *Indian Love Poems* (Knopf/Random House/Everyman); 'Winter' in The *Literary Review* and *Yellow Nib*; 'Kargil' in *Platform*, *Yellow Nib*, *Caravan*, *Australian Poetry Journal* and *Ladakh* (Tyrone Guthrie Centre / Gallerie); 'One Moonlit December Night' in *Indian Love Poems* (Penguin); 'Prayer Flag' in *World Literature Today*; 'Indian Dessert' and ' Desire' in *Leela: An Erotic Play of Verse and Art* (Collins); 'Line-Breaks' and 'Over May Day' in *Out of Bounds* (Bloodaxe); 'Mediterranean' in *New Writing 15* (Granta); and 'Woman with Amphora' was a prize winner at the British Council All India Poetry Competition.

🦌

DEDICATIONS

The following poems were originally dedicated to various people: 'Banyan' for Jane Draycott; 'Rabindranath Tagore' for William Butler Yeats; 'Chinese Calligraphy' for Wang Anyi, Zhao Lihong, Peihua & Su De; 'Ophelia: Bacterial Fragments' for Kim Morrissey; 'Grammar' for M Dolores Herrero (Loli); 'Lily Pads' for Indrajit Hazra; 'Aorta Art' for Arjun Kalyanpur; 'Matrix' for Priya Sarukkai Chabria; 'Goa Haiku' for Janet Pierce; 'Tongue: Diptych' for Joseph Brodsky & Mark Strand; 'New Public Library' for Benjamin Law & Kirsty Murray; 'Safe' for Chandrahas Choudhury; 'Postcards' for Dom Moraes & Basu Bhattacharyya; 'Rain' for Camille Lizarribar; 'Stills from Sanskriti' for Jenny Lewis; 'Prayer Flag' for Deb & Purobi Mukharji; 'Blue' for Iman Mersal; 'Silence' for Anuradha Sehgal; 'Mohiniyattam' for Bharati Shivaji & Vijayalakshmi; 'Bharatanatyam Dancer' for Leela Samson; 'Odissi' for Madhavi Mudgal; 'Almost a Touch' for Navtej Johar & Sunil Mehra; 'Dedication' for Kun-Yang Lin; 'MH-17 Crash' for Malachi Edwin Vethamani & Eddin Khoo; 'Four Watercolours' for Alan Ross

& Jane Rye; 'Cover Drawing' for Imtiaz Dharker; 'Cow-Dust Hour' for Rokeya Sultana; 'Gaayika'r Chithi: Notes from a Singer's Scoresheet' for Shama Rahman; 'English Colours' for Paul & Susan Utting; 'Shadows of Black', 'Moth Art' and 'Feast' for Manisha Gera Baswani; 'Acrylic' for Zita & Mustaque Ahmed; 'Anish Kapoor' for Anish Kapoor; 'Yuki' for Bina Sarkar & Rafeeq Ellias; 'Red Rain' for Tanvir Fattah & Kelley Lynch; 'Iris' for Iris Murdoch & John Bayley; 'Freehold|Leasehold' for K S Radhakrishnan & Mini; 'Entropy' for Megan Randall; 'Your Flight' for Frances Kiernan; 'Crossing Tongues' for Moon Jung Hee, Cho Dong Hoi, Kim Ku Sul, Choi Hae Ok & Walter Lew; 'Ledig Notes' for D W Gibson; 'Macedonian Triptych' for Zoran & Beba; 'Electric Text' for Seamus Heaney; 'Changing Hands' for Louis & Robert Gault; 'Guinness' for Derek Walcott; 'Ballynahinch' for Louis & Aria; 'The Wailing Wall' for Yehuda Amichai; 'Desert Triptych' for Danielle Schaub; 'Diaspora' for Dan Daor & Amir Or; 'Carving Salmon' for Zoran Anchevski; 'Almaya, Jaffa' for Ya'ir Dalal; 'Reading with the Wind' for Tsur & Dorit Shezaf; 'Striking Matches' for Adil Jussawalla; 'Necklace' for Riva Ganguly Das; 'Mirrorwork' for Mimi Khalvati; 'Facsimile' for Kwame Dawes, 'Dadu' for Didu; 'Suspended Particles' for Jacqueline Bardolph; 'During the Street Play' for Safdar Hashmi; 'Elegy for Delhi: 29/10' for U R Ananthamurthy, Arun Kolatkar, Kunwar Narain, Anamika & K Satchidanandan; 'Baba' for Ma; 'Ma' for Baba; 'Mother' for Peter, Anna & Elizabeth Walcott; 'The Photograph' for Susheila Nasta; 'Fragmented Feathers and Transparent Bones' for Aamer Hussein; 'Rhyme Royal for an Ancient Chinese Wine' for Vikram Seth; 'Sexless like Alphabets' for Joseph Brodsky & Maria Sozzani; 'Birch' for Aaron Taylor; 'Valley of the Gods' for Amitav Ghosh; 'Rosary of Waves' for Douglas Livingstone; '97 6th Avenue, Mayfair' for Stephen Gray; 'Remembering Hiroshima Tonight' for Phillis Levin; 'Neonic Cocktail' for Jayanta Mahapatra; 'Asylum' for William Matthews & David Ignatow; 'Leaning Against the Lamp-Post' for Suman Gupta; 'Lord Jagannath' for Prafulla Mohanty; 'A Pilgrimage to Mathura' for Leela Gandhi; 'August 9, 1964' for Ma & Baba; 'Sun's Golden Sands' for Aftab Seth, Romi Chopra & Gopal Gandhi; 'Bowl' for Janice Pariat, Luigi Russi & Manisha Bhattacharya; and 'Translating Poetry' for Amarjit Chandan & A K Ramanujan.

෴

THANK YOU

A massive book project like this one ultimately has to be a labour of passion. And for that passion and love to be fulfilled, many along the way have lent their quiet support over the last few decades. Thank you to:

— Bina Sarkar Ellias of Gallerie Publishers, Jeremy Poynting of Peepal Tree Press, and Bryce Milligan of Wings Press for their belief in this book as a whole. Arvind Lodaya of Lodaya|Design+Consulting for unflinchingly and super efficiently translating my master book and cover design into elegant typeset pages and cover. Also to M E H Haider, Ramesh Bharti & Sanjeev Gupta for pre-press preparations; and Sanjay Varma of Star Publications.

— the literary editors and publishers who have commissioned me to edit or curate special issues/portfolios of Indian literature/poetry or anthologies. All those projects, ideal preparatory work for this book, have helped this anthology to be a better one. I'd like to put on record the names of the following editors: Peter Forbes and Fiona Sampson (*Poetry Review*, UK), Djelal Kadir, William Riggan and Daniel Simon (*World Literature Today*, USA), Ciaran Carson and Ed Larissy (*Yellow Nib*, Seamus Heaney Centre for Poetry at Queens University, Belfast), Ilya Kaminsky, Christian Wiman, Don Share & Beth Allen (Poetry Foundation, Chicago / *Poetry* magazine), Kwame Dawes (*Prairie Schooner*, USA), Tessa Ransford (*Lines Review*, Edinburgh), David & Helen Constantine (*Modern Poetry in Translation*, UK), Ursula Owen and Judith Vidal-Hall (*Index for Censorship*, UK), Susheila Nasta (*Wasafiri*, UK), Zoran Anchevski (commissioning editor & translator, *Midnight's Grandchildren*, Struga Macedonia), Walter Cummins, Thomas Kennedy and Minna Proctor (*The Literary Review*, USA), Adonis [Ali Ahmad Said Asbar] and Osama Esber (*The Other*, Damascus/Paris), David Shook (*Molossus*, USA), James Byrne (*The Wolf*, London/New York), Kavita Jindal (*Writer's Hub*, London), Brinda Datta (*Biblio*, New Delhi), Catriona Mitchell & Nic Low (AsiaLink 'The Bookwallah', Australia), David Lehman, Stacey Harwood & Catherine Woodward (*The Best American Poetry*), and others.

— the judges of various committees who awarded me fellowships, visitorships and residencies (and others who helped in that process) where parts of this book was worked upon: late Sir Stephen Spender, Christopher Reid [Faber & Faber ex-poetry editor], Jonathan Galassi [Farrar Strauss Giroux literary editor], John Casey, Caroline Moore, The Lord Briggs, The Earl of Perth, The Lord Quinton, The Lord Weidenfeld, Sir Steven Runciman, Adam Czernawski, and Drue Heinz [*The Paris Review* publisher] for the Hawthornden Fellowship (UK); Pat Donlon, Janet Pierce and Patrick MacCabe (Tyrone Guthrie Centre, Ireland); D W Gibson (Ledig House, New York); Prabhu Guptara (Wolfsberg UBS, Switzerland); Chandrika Grover (Pro Helvetia Swiss Arts Council, New Delhi); Henk Propper and Thomas Mohlmann (NLPVF Dutch Foundation for Literature, Amsterdam); O P Jain (Sanskriti, New Delhi); Wang Anyi and Hu Peihua (Shanghai Writers Programme, China); Clare Morgan and Jane Draycott (Oxford University); John Kinsella (Cambridge University); Douglas Dunn and Robert Crawford (St Andrews University); John Thieme (University of Hull); Susheila Nasta (Queen Mary & Westfield College); Dennis Walder (Open University); John Siddique (Judge, 'Stanza Poetry Prize', Poetry Society of UK); George Szirtes (East Anglia University); William Radice (SOAS London University); Linda Hess (Stanford University); Graham Huggan (Harvard University); and finally, the committee members of the Government of India Ministry of Culture who awarded me the senior fellowship for "outstanding persons in the field of culture/literature".

— my publishers & editors: Jon Philips, John Welch, Jeremy Poynting, Bryce Milligan, Leona Medlin, R K Mehra, Nirupam Chatterjee, Renuka Chaterjee, Sanjana Roy Choudhury, Chandana Dutta, Bipin Shah, Bina Sarkar Ellias, Arpita Das, V K Karthika, Shantanu Ray Chaudhuri, Ananth Padmanabhan,

Milee Ashwarya, Meru Gokhale, Udayan Mitra, Caroline Newbury, Hemali Sodhi, Neha Punj, Rachna Pratap, Neelima P Aryan, Ahlawat Gunjan, Shatarupa Ghoshal, Nazaqat Ahamed.

— A K Ramanujan, Dom Moraes, Nissim Ezekiel, Jayanta Mahapatra, Adil Jussawalla, Keki Daruwalla, Shiv K Kumar, Agha Shahid Ali, Amitav Ghosh, Vikram Seth, Shashi Tharoor, Amit Chaudhuri, Ravi Shankar, Arundhati Subramaniam, Priya Sarukkai Chabria, Tabish Khair, Daljit Nagra, Imtiaz Dharker, Meena Alexander, Leela Gandhi, Chitra Banerjee Divakaruni, Arshia Sattar, Anamika, Aminur Rahman, Tulsi Badrinath, Chandrahas Choudhury, K Satchidanandan, Gulzar,

— Peter Porter, Daniel Weissbort, George Szirtes, Alan Jenkins, Carol Ann Duffy, Fiona Sampson, Maureen Duffy, Elaine Feinstein, Ruth Padel, Glyn Maxwell, Jane Draycott, Jenny Lewis, Lesley Saunders, Kim Morrissey, Paul Nandi, Aamer Hussein, Sunetra Gupta, Stephen Watts, Leona Medlin, Sandeep Parmar, Mona Arshi, James Byrne, Todd Swift, Bernardine Evaristo, Maggie Gee, Ruth Borthwick, Melanie Abrahams, Michael Walling,

— Joseph Brodsky, Derek Walcott & Sigrid Nama, Les Murray, Donald Hall, Charles Bernstein, William Matthews, David Ignatow, Phillis Levin, Kwame Dawes, Colin Channer, Wendy Barker, Fred D'Aguiar,

— Dan Daor & Gaby Silon, Amir Or, Tsur & Dorit Shezaf, Ya'ir Dalal, Mark & Sara Sofer, Eli & Yael, Sharon Rappaport, Zoran Anchevski, Iztok Osojnik, Hans van der Waarsenburg, Ciaran O' Driscoll, John Davies, Alan & Prajna; Aurelia & Julian, Anastassis & Maria, H.E. Dame Pearlette Louisy, Peter, Anna & Elizabeth Walcott,

— Malashri & Robey Lal, Alka Pande, Shormishtha Panja, Rama Nair, Leela Samson, Aftab Seth, Pavan Varma, Bharati Shivaji & Vijaylakshmi, Shovana Narayan, Amal Chatterjee & Susan Ridder, Marlisse Mensink & Bauke Steenstra, Deb & Purobi Mukharji, Pinak & Radha Chakravarty, Riva Ganguly & Proshanto Das, Probir Sen, Gopal & Tara Gandhi, Aftab Seth, Romi Chopra,

— Ma & Baba (who sadly did not live to see the finished bound copy of this book), Didu, Mama, Maj'uncle, Bubumashi, and my dear cousins: Babua, Chotto, Bulbuli, Mithun & Tukun — all your support, calm and love have been invaluable.

— Aria, my dearest son, for putting up with all the time away from you — travelling, photographing, researching and writing — you are my guiding star, strength and eternal love.

I take responsibility for any unwarranted errors in the book, but all praise should go to the people for their support of my work. And apologies if I have inadvertently left out any names in this list. My gratitude and love to you all.

— SUDEEP SEN
New Delhi

THE LONDON MAGAZINE

— EST. 1732 —

LONDON MAGAZINE EDITIONS

THE LONDON MAGAZINE
——— EST. 1732 ———

HISTORY

ENGLAND'S OLDEST LITERARY PERIODICAL was founded in 1732 as *The London Magazine*, or *Gentleman's Monthly Intelligencer*, a rival to the new and popular, *Gentleman's Magazine*.

Revived in 1820 by a new editor, John Scott, the Magazine went on to publish work by the leaders of a rising generation of English romantics. In September 1821, the first two instalments of Thomas De Quincey's *Confessions of an English Opium Eater* appeared in the Magazine. Charles Lamb, Leigh Hunt, and Thomas Carlyle were also contributors. John Scott died in a duel in 1821. An associate of John Gibson Lockhart, editor of Blackwood's Magazine, shot him in the stomach. His death was the culmination of a long rivalry between the two. Publication ceased in 1829.

The magazine restarted in 1898 under the ownership of the Harmsworth brothers, famous for starting the *Daily Mail* in 1896 and the *Daily Mirror* in 1903. Editorship was given to younger brother Cecil, who embraced the undertaking with gusto. In February 1903, H. G. Wells published his first short story for the Magazine, *Mr Skelmersdale in Fairyland*. In the following years he was included in the publication several more times, including an article specially commissioned by Harmsworth in 1908, entitled *The Things that Live on Mars*.

During the early twentieth century, *The London Magazine* also published original stories from the likes of Arthur Conan Doyle, Joseph Conrad, Jack London, and P. G. Wodehouse. A short story by E. Nesbit was included in almost every issue of 1904, and her most famous novel, *The Railway Children*, was serialised in the magazine the year before its commercial release in 1906. Thomas Hardy was also published in the Magazine, and famous illustrator W. Heath Robinson contributed several original prints. In 1933, the Magazine closed again.

In 1954, editor and writer John Lehmann founded the most recent incarnation of *The London Magazine*: it has been published continuously since. In the first issue, T. S. Eliot recommended to readers "a magazine that will boldly assume the existence of a public interested in serious literature…". Louis MacNeice published his *Canto In Memoriam Dylan Thomas*, and Henry Green reviewed the diaries of Virginia Woolf.

Under Lehmann, and subsequent editors Alan Ross (who became editor in 1961 for forty years) and Sebastian Barker (2001), the Magazine became a pole star in the London literary firmament, developing a reputation for publishing the best and most interesting fiction, poetry, criticism and essays from England and across the world, and for helping to bring a new of a generation of young English writers to public attention.

Across a long life — spanning several incarnations – the pages of the Magazine have played host to a wide range of canonical writers, from Percy Bysshe Shelley, William Wordsworth, William Hazlitt and John Keats in the 18th-century, to T.S. Eliot, W.H. Auden, T S Eliot, Sylvia Plath, Dylan Thomas and Evelyn Waugh in the early 20th-century.

Its writers on 'art' have included John Richardson, Alan Bowness, Edward Lucie-Smith and Mel Gooding and it has featured original work by Graham Sutherland, Prunella Clough, Maggie Hambling and Frank Auerbach.

Meanwhile, in recent decades the Magazine has published work by giants of contemporary fiction and poetry such as Doris Lessing, William Burroughs, Harold Pinter, William Boyd, Les Murray, Paul Muldoon, Nadine Gordimer and Derek Walcott.

Now, *The London Magazine* is re-launched under the editorship of Steven O'Brien. Here is a magazine re-invigorated for the twenty-first-century, which — just like the city from which it takes its name — combines a rich history with a fiercely contemporary outlook, and which draws together ideas, and voices, from across the globe. Eclectic in taste, promiscuously interested and unapologetically intelligent, *The London Magazine* continues to publish the best writing from London and the wider world.

LONDON MAGAZINE EDITIONS

Founded by Editor Alan Ross in 1965, TLM Editions
is the in-house publishing arm of *The London Magazine*.
In our continuing commitment to seeking out
the most original and promising voices
in contemporary poetry and prose,
TLM Editions works closely with its writers
to produce books which are diverse, intelligent and imaginative.

SELECTED NEW TITLES & BACKLIST:
Making for the Exit by Edward Lucie-Smith
Goodbye Crocodile by Conor Patrick
Degrees of Twilight by Maggie Butt
Tales of Survival: Caribbean Stories and Poems by Davis Deen
Fractals by Sudeep Sen

The Lioners by Tony Harrison
Cape Drives by Christopher Hope
Private and Confidential by Herbert Lomas
Six Epistles to Eva Hesse by Donald Davie
The Pleasures of Flesh by Gavin Ewart
Mr Maui by Peter Bland
Interior by Brian Jones
Rhine Jump by Geoffrey Holloway
Day and Night by Ronald Botrall
Sabon Gari by John Haynes
Eight Colours Wide by Deborah Tall
With the Volume Turned Down by Reiner Kunze
They Killed Sitting Bull by Gunnar Harding
Collected Poems by Bernard Spencer
The Window Game by John Normanton
The Flying Men by Patricia Whittaker
Old Damson-Face by Bernard Gutteridge
Reflections on the Nile by Ronald Bottrall
Afterimages by Shinkichi Takahashi
Peru: The New Poetry by David Tipton
Demons Don't by Robert Conquest
The Taj Express by Alan Ross
The Reign of Sparrows by Roy Fuller
Night Vision by Tomas Transtromer